MONUMENTS MATTER

MONUMENTS MATTER

INDIA'S ARCHAEOLOGICAL HERITAGE SINCE INDEPENDENCE

Nayanjot Lahiri

Marg

Editors
JYOTINDRA JAIN
NAMAN P. AHUJA

Senior Editorial Executive
ARNAVAZ K. BHANSALI
Assistant Editors
SUCHETA CHAKRABORTY
MRINALINI VASUDEVAN

Text Editor (Consultant)
RIVKA ISRAEL

Designer
NAJU HIRANI

Senior Production Executive
GAUTAM V. JADHAV
Production Executive
CHETAN S. MORE

Vol. 68 No. 4 June 2017
Price: ₹ 2800.00 / US$ 69.95
ISBN: 978-93-83243-17-4
Library of Congress Catalog Card Number: 2017-322021

Published by Radhika Sabavala for The Marg Foundation at Army & Navy Building (3rd Floor), 148, M.G. Road, Mumbai 400 001, India.
Processed at The Marg Foundation, Mumbai.
Printed at Silverpoint Press Pvt. Ltd., Navi Mumbai.

Page 1: (clockwise from top) Scene from the Chhadanta Jataka; Double humped camels on the coping stone of a railing; Pedestal of an image (possibly the standing Buddha found in its vicinity), at Kanaganahalli, Gulbarga district, Karnataka.
Page 3: Excavations at Sarnath, May 2014.
Pages 4 and 5: Story of Udayana; Mulakasethi carrying his son in an entourage; King Pulumavi bequeathing Ujjain to Ajayata; Dharmachakra on a drum slab of the Maha stupa at Kanaganahalli, Gulbarga district, Karnataka.
Photographs: Nayanjot Lahiri.

Marg's quarterly publications receive support from Tata Trusts

Contents

Prelude and Acknowledgements

This is a book about the state of India's archaeological heritage since independence. It owes its genesis to Vidya Dehejia who in December 2012, when she was general editor of Marg, invited me to do a volume on the various issues that, as she put it, "affect or are related to Indian archaeology". Her email communicated that the trigger for this invitation had been an article that I had written in a national newspaper on the sorry state of the protected Buddhist site of Kanaganahalli in Karnataka ("Hold Fast to the Past", *Hindustan Times*, October 26, 2012). After that initial invitation, it took time to put together this volume because of another book that I was then in the process of writing, since published as *Ashoka in Ancient India* (2015). Kanaganahalli figures in that book as well as the present one, and photographs of the site and its extraordinary sculpture grace the cover and preliminary pages of this book.

The book has been written on the assumption that 70 years is a substantial enough time frame to undertake a stocktaking of the achievements of, and the challenges that have confronted, the world of Indian archaeology since independence. Apart from a range of field research, the book looks at institutions that make up the archaeological establishment, in which the Archaeological Survey of India (ASI) looms large. There is a reason for this. While India possesses a very large government machinery whose responsibilities range from research to the management and preservation of India's monuments, the juggernaut among departments and directorates of archaeology and museums is the ASI that is attached to the Union Ministry of Culture. The ASI has a reasonably distinguished history of institutional research going back to 1861, and since the early 20th century, it has been the premier body responsible for the conservation, preservation and maintenance of monuments. It is not surprising that the lion's share—roughly a third—of the Ministry's annual budget (Plan and Non-Plan) goes to the ASI.

Apart from institutions, the work of a range of individuals also figures in the book, largely in the endnotes. Among the many names that appear here are university men and women, antiquarians and government archaeologists including the first woman Director General of the ASI, Debala Mitra. Important discoveries, incidentally, have also frequently been made because of the interest and commitment of individual researchers who were not necessarily institutional academics. The discovery of rock art in the state of Madhya Pradesh is an example of this. Here, the names that come to mind are people like V.S. Wakankar, the itinerant scholar who discovered Bhimbetka, and the school teacher J.D. Tripathi who devoted his life to discovering and documenting the paintings of Narsinghgarh. Another school teacher, Manicklal Singha from Bishnupur in Bengal, spent most of his weekends visiting and collecting from archaeological sites, eventually building up the first museum of Bankura district. While this volume is not a comprehensive history of Indian archaeology since independence, it is perhaps necessary to remember that as and when that is written, the world outside academia will form part of the story in much the same way as it did in the 19th century.

The book begins with the dawn of independence and partition. Because the story of the fate of monuments and museum collections in the aftermath of 1947, in what is best described as an unprecedented situation of turbulence and trauma, is hardly known, there is a strong historical narrative there. The book then moves on to impart a sense of the cumulative archaeological research from 1947 till the first decade of the present century. Apart from an overview of field research that unearthed cultural remains across millennia, some new techniques and their impact in changing our understanding of the pattern of settlements in ancient India are also considered. What happens to monuments and archaeological sites forms the other segment of this book. How do sites get protected, who gets them protected, why do many of them come under pressure or get destroyed—these are among the issues that are explored. Some of these issues are less widely known than others, especially since they frequently remain buried in government files. The role of political leadership in promoting archaeology (especially in the early years of independence), individual initiatives and community practices that help in preserving monuments, the nature and impact of the performance audits of government-funded cultural institutions (ranging from the ASI to museums) conducted by the Comptroller and Auditor General's Office, the interventions of parliamentary committees—these are also matters discussed here. Finally, the legal interventions around archaeological monuments and sites are examined. Naturally, the ramifications of the legal dispute around the Babri Masjid and its destruction at Ayodhya, especially since a court-directed excavation was ordered there for the first time in India's history, is discussed.

India's material heritage forms an irreplaceable archive of past human activity, of the achievements and processes through which we became who we are. Equally, like our natural heritage, it is awfully endangered. This is true for many parts of the world and certainly for India where, as a people, our pride in our heritage is always surplus while caring for that heritage suffers a huge deficit. In the case of the natural heritage, because of a vast and vigilant non-governmental organizational network, there is greater awareness and action on the ground. This book, it is hoped, will help in spreading some awareness about the magnitude of the problems even while it cannot offer any clear-cut solutions to how these can be tackled.

In putting together this volume, there are many debts that have accumulated along the way. There are scholars who have contributed ideas and photographs: Parth R. Chauhan (Chandigarh), Dilip Khamari (ASI, Chhattisgarh), Ravi Korisettar (Dharwad), Abdul Rashid Lone (Srinagar), S.B. Ota (ASI, New Delhi), Shanti Pappu (Chennai), K. Rajan (Pondicherry), M.B. Rajani (Bengaluru), Upinder Singh (New Delhi), Prakash Sinha (Allahabad), V.H. Sonawane (Baroda), Sila Tripathi (Goa) and Rakesh Tiwari, Director General of the ASI (who gave permission to use the large number of photographs from the ASI albums that are reproduced here, and those pertaining to his own work in Uttar Pradesh). There are Kishore and Karan Lahiri who have substantially contributed to the chapter "Our Heritage and the Law". There is the outstanding team at Marg that has kept its faith in me, especially the present editors Jyotindra Jain and Naman Ahuja.

Above all, there is Kuldip Singh, the architect and collector, with whom I have connections of all kinds. He is my paternal uncle (Chachaji) and, he is also the first truly cerebral person in my family with whom I have had the good fortune of sharing a lifelong relationship. For as long as I can remember, he has imparted to me a sense of the enormous pleasures involved in exploring ideas and books, monuments and artefacts. For the joy of walking and talking with him about everything under the sun, and for the sheer force of his example, this book is dedicated to him.

Architectural remains at Kanaganahalli, Gulbarga district, Karnataka. Photograph: Nayanjot Lahiri.

1 Independence and Partition

"Independence Day" dawned on August 15, 1947 as a day of national celebrations. These began on August 14 itself when the Constituent Assembly of India, mandated with the task of drafting a constitution, held a special session at 11 pm. Prime Minister Jawaharlal Nehru was the star speaker there, his words imparting a strong sense of occasion. "At the stroke of the midnight hour when the world sleeps," Nehru announced, "India will awake to life and freedom." As members of the Assembly listened to the chimes that marked the "midnight hour", one of them blew a conchshell to welcome independence. Thousands crowded around the entrance of the Council building (now Sansad Bhavan, the Parliament House) where the Assembly held its session. Across India, festive lights and the national flag adorned shopping centres, public buildings, homes and religious shrines.

August 15, 1947 also saw a redrawing of the political map as a consequence of which a united India came to be partitioned into the two nation-states of India and Pakistan. Partition was accompanied by a horrific bloodbath resulting in more than a million dead, and a two-way mass migration involving several million people. Where and how refugee populations were rehabilitated, the mechanism for land compensation, the partitioning of resources, the trauma of displacement and death in the aftermath of August 1947—these are issues that have figured in the vast documentary material generated by those events, from first-person accounts of the times to histories written after the dust had settled. What have not been considered in the same way are the pressures and problems that the subcontinent's archaeological past had to face on account of the demographic deluge on the one hand, and the division of assets on the other.

This chapter examines independence and partition in relation to India's heritage. As the country divested itself of British rule, what was the impact on monuments, museums and research? How did the Archaeological Survey of India deal with the challenges posed by those turbulent years? How did India's political leadership respond to the challenges? I look at several

1.1 and 1.2 Plaques on the Plassey Memorial in the early part of the 20th century. Courtesy ASI.

of these issues while exploring the brunt and the burden of the aftermath of 1947 on India's architectural and archaeological heritage.

The Fate of Monuments

The end of the British Raj and the creation of the nation-states of India and Pakistan impacted the character of monuments in at least four different ways. First, there were attacks on certain monuments that were seen as embodying the brutal character of British rule. Second, several monuments of the British era were sought to be changed by the British authorities themselves. Third, in certain instances, statues that had been put up by the British in public places in India were removed and relocated by the Indian government. Finally, the turbulence of partition triggered attacks on mosques, tombs and shrines even as some of them were converted into large refugee camps.

The attacks on monuments began on August 15 itself, and were initially aimed at those perceived as symbols of British colonial oppression. Monuments that memorialized foundational moments of the colonial era were specifically targeted—in a large swathe stretching from Krishnanagar in West Bengal to Kanpur in the United Provinces (now Uttar Pradesh). The Battle of Plassey site was one such memorial that saw a big demonstration on August 15. Plassey is the Anglicized form of Palashi, the name of a small town on the highway that leads from Kolkata to Murshidabad. It was in the fields and orchards beyond the town that a battle was fought on June 23, 1757 between the British East India Company force directed by Robert Clive and Siraj-ud-Daulah, the nawab of Bengal. The actual battle had been a somewhat minor campaign but was memorialized by the British as a major military victory in establishing their rule in India. What made matters worse was the fact that the memorial was prolifically inscribed in language that evoked the image of a major and prolonged encounter—with a plaque that even provided details of the membership of the "Council of War of Plassey" (figures 1.1 and 1.2). Indians, on the other hand, viewed Plassey as a battle won by

the British through treachery rather than military prowess, thanks to the intrigues of Clive with deceivers and plotters like Mir Jafar, the commander-in-chief of the nawab's army. A campaign of protest against the memorial began on August 15 when the demonstrators, describing it as a national disgrace, inflicted minor damage on it and demanded that it be entirely removed. The demand for its removal was evidently a way of underscoring political independence from those who had set it up.[1]

In Kanpur too, a mob gathered at what used to be called the Memorial Well complex. It was this well into which, during the 1857 uprising against the British, many bodies of Europeans, murdered on the instructions of the rebel leader Nana Sahib, had been thrown. A memorial was erected here in 1863 by the British government, consisting of a marble angel on the wellhead, while the well, set in the centre of the garden, came to be surrounded by an elaborate Gothic arch. An inscription set out the details of this event, and there were also

various tombs in the complex, of those killed in the revolt. In the years following the suppression of the revolt, Indians were admitted to the garden on the payment of an entrance fee, while admission to the well and the tombs was banned. Only "Europeans" were permitted there. Now, at independence, a large mob invaded the areas from which Indians had been kept out. Protestors blackened the face of the marble angel on the wellhead, broke its hands, and desecrated some of the graves.[2]

How did the government deal with attacks on monuments and demands for their removal? At Plassey, on the advice of N.P. Chakravarti who had succeeded Mortimer Wheeler as the Director General of the ASI in 1948, a gesture towards modifying the memorial was made: the plaques, with the exception of the one giving the date of the battle, were removed. At Kanpur, an entirely different set of events unfolded. Although the United Provinces government carried out repairs, the future of Kanpur's Memorial Well became the subject of anxious and urgent consideration for the United Kingdom High Commission in India. After a great deal of discussion with the local Christian

organizations, the High Commission decided that the angel, along with a screen and tombstones, would be shifted to the churchyard of the All Souls Memorial Church in the complex (figure 1.3). But in order to ensure that the old site was not attacked in future, it was decided that the entire area would be levelled so as to leave no trace of its former significance (figure 1.4). As Brigadier Bullock, who was in charge of the British Monuments and Graves Section of the High Commission, underlined, all steps were to be taken to ensure that "the losing of the identity" of the actual site was done so thoroughly that no future visitor would be able to say where the well had been.[3]

A majority of British monuments, incidentally, remained unscathed post-1947. However, and this is the second point that requires reiteration, there were changes of another kind which related to their maintenance as a consequence of policy decisions in England. Take the case of graves and tombstones. In an announcement to both Houses of Parliament on March 15, 1949, the British government stated that it was impossible to undertake a full-scale maintenance of all cemeteries in

1.5 and 1.6 All that remains of the Rajpura Cemetery in Delhi is a gateway and a badly spat-upon memorial stone. Photographs: Nayanjot Lahiri.

India and Pakistan. Some 45,000 pounds used to be spent annually on the maintenance of cemeteries through the Indian Ecclesiastical Establishment. The Establishment was replaced by the British Monuments and Graves Section of the British High Commissioner's Office, when it soon became evident that substantial reductions in cemetery expenditure would have to be made. Importantly, as the parliamentary announcement stated, while London would try to maintain several of them (especially the more important of the historical cemeteries) through a limited commitment, in cases "where they could not be maintained…they should revert to nature in a dignified and decent manner".[4] Evidently, fiscal logic was the primary cause for the "abandonment" of several "minor" British graves and monuments in India. The Rajpura Cemetery in the University of Delhi appears to be one such place, where the original cemetery has disappeared, and parts of it have been built over by an illegal Christian Colony. All the graves in the cemetery that still exist are of post-1971 vintage, with only a gateway and a badly spat-upon memorial stone reminding us of what was originally there (figures 1.5 and 1.6).

At a third level, in the 1960s, the Indian government took the initiative in removing a large number of statues from prominent public places. The idea was that since these were colonial symbols, they ought to be removed from public sight. This was similar to the changes that took place in relation to other "anti-national" symbols such as the British names of roads. In Calcutta, for instance, just days before independence, Clive Street had been renamed Netaji Subhas Road. In Delhi, while the British names of roads were not initially removed, statues were, and fairly comprehensively, from those of British viceroys to King George V himself. The king's statue used to stand under the canopy opposite India Gate and was relocated to Coronation Park in north Delhi. The statue of John Nicholson, the British "hero" of the Delhi assault (known to history as a particularly brutal commander), was also removed from what used to be called the Nicholson Gardens near Kashmere Gate. Post-independence, this was taken down and relocated to his old school, Royal School Dungannon, in Northern Ireland. Statues were removed in Calcutta as well, and many of these were placed in the gardens of Flagstaff House in Barrackpore.

Similarly, in Uttar Pradesh, statues of Queen Victoria were taken out of public places and several of these can still be seen, dumped in the backyard of the state museum at Mathura. Not all the larger-than-life figures of British rulers and viceroys, though, were relegated to such backyards. In fact, in places like Madras (now Chennai) and at Bangalore (now Bengaluru), there are still statues standing in their original surroundings. At Cubbon Park in Bengaluru, for instance, there is the larger-than-life Queen Victoria, the statue of King Edward VII and also that of the man who the park was named after, Major General Sir Mark Cubbon himself.

The winding up of British rule in 1947 was one part of the political story that impacted monuments. The other, and infinitely more traumatic, set of events emanated from the redrawing and partitioning of the subcontinent's political map. The impact of the partition on historic landscapes is the fourth and final aspect that I explore here.

Religious monuments in several parts of India and Pakistan were under siege in 1947. In Pakistan, we do know, for instance, about many gurdwaras which were attacked and occupied in the aftermath of partition. Iqbal Qaiser's book *Historical Sikh Shrines in Pakistan* mentions many such cases, including Gurdwara Chota Nanakiana at Manga whose building was burnt down in 1947, Gurdwara Chowbachcha Sahib at Dharampura which came to be occupied by refugee families from north and central India, and Gurdwara Manjhi Sahib at Manakdeke which continues to house families descended from Mewat refugees who first inhabited it after partition.[5] However, since the focus of this book is on India, it is the fate of the monuments on this side of the border which will be discussed in some detail.

Pressures on monuments came from looters, from refugee camps, as also from the callous acts of omission and commission of various government departments. Delhi is an example

1.7 The minarets in this photograph of the Moti Masjid in Delhi are those that were subsequently built. The original minarets were destroyed in 1947. Photograph: Nayanjot Lahiri.

1.8 Shah Alam's tomb in Wazirabad before partition. Courtesy ASI.

1.9 Shah Alam's tomb as it appears today—without the grave inside the tomb and without the jalis. Photograph: Nayanjot Lahiri.

of this. It was in September 1947 that the capital became the site of a particularly vicious campaign in which Muslims were butchered by the thousands, and in its wake symbols of Muslim culture such as tombs and mosques were attacked. The scale of the damage is vividly documented in the ASI files: the manner in which Mehrauli's Moti Masjid had its marble minars torn off (figure 1.7); the demolishing of four tombs in the crypt of Sultan Ghari and the unsuccessful attempt to convert it into a temple; the same intention at the Chauburji Masjid on the Delhi Ridge where, in fact, a cement Hanuman came to be set up (to be eventually removed with police help); the destruction of the grave of Shah Alam at Wazirabad, and of red sandstone jalis surrounding it (figures 1.8 and 1.9); and a great deal else.[6]

If in Delhi looters targeted mosques and tombs, in some states, it was the administration that oversaw more organized campaigns of destruction. In the princely states of Alwar and Bharatpur in 1947, mosques and tombs were targeted under the orders of the government with specific contracts being given for demolition. The profit to be made by grabbing the land on which these stood was the primary motive of demolition. The quoted confidential report below, by an ASI officer Shankar Das, underlined this in the case of Alwar:

I visited Alwar on 10th December 1947, and studied the demolition of the mosques, graveyards and tombs in and around the city. This demolition campaign was launched by the state during the last disturbance and is still going on at some places. The State Ministers after a conference entrusted the task of demolition to one Sardar Joginder Singh, S.D.O. of the Public Works Department. This S.D.O. summoned various contractors and distributed the mosques and tombs for demolition amongst them on the simple conditions that whatever building material was got out of the debris would be appropriated by the contractor and virgin soil over which such a structure stood would be forfeited to the State. The contractors lost no time in razing both the old and new mosques as well as graveyards to the ground....[7]

1.10 An illustration showing the mosque in the premises of the Gumbad Fateh Jang, Alwar, which was demolished after partition. Courtesy ASI.

Consequently, the singular brackets and balcony chhajjas (projecting eaves) of the Gumbad Fateh Jang in Alwar were pulled down and the mosque situated in its northern enclosure was dismantled (figures 1.10 and 1.11). That the Gumbad survived was because refugees from Pakistan persuaded the contractor that they be allowed to stay there till suitable accommodation was found elsewhere.

As the case of Gumbad Fateh Jang reveals, even as Islamic monuments came under attack, they simultaneously provided refugees with much-needed shelter. Initially, it was Muslims seeking a safe haven who occupied such places. In Delhi, camps were set up in monuments like Purana Qila, Feroz Shah Kotla, Humayun's Tomb and Safdarjung's Tomb. Later, tens of thousands of Hindu and Sikh refugees took shelter in such camps, which continued to exist for several years after partition.

Exceptional times evidently required exceptional measures. This is perhaps why the ASI chose to ignore, for humanitarian reasons, what was stipulated in the act governing monuments and archaeological sites—that the monuments protected by it could not be occupied. Instead, it agreed to a more ethical option: while permitting some of the monuments to be used as temporary refugee camps with tents pitched within the compounds, it laid down certain conditions—only allowing minor alterations which could later be removed without in any way damaging the character of the monuments (figures 1.12 and 1.13). These conditions, however, could rarely be enforced.

An instance that vividly demonstrates the humanitarian issues and challenges faced in those times is the case of Sher Shah's Mosque in Purana Qila (figures 1.14 and 1.15). In April 1948, the Ministry of Relief and Rehabilitation wrote to the rehabilitation commissioner about the need to accommodate a primary school for refugee children in the mosque. Some 7000 people were living in the camp at Purana Qila, with 500 children being taught by the refugees themselves in open-air classes—a situation which, with the summer of 1948 approaching,

could not be sustained. When this letter was forwarded to Mortimer Wheeler, Director General of the ASI, he made it clear that while other parts of the historic fort could be used, the unique character of the mosque made it impossible to hand it over for a primary school. As he pleaded, "It is quite impossible for my Department to authorize the use of the Sher Shah Mosque as indicated. This mosque is an architectural gem of the highest value, and occupies a particularly high place in the history of Indo-Muslim culture."[8] Wheeler's plea fell on deaf ears. The mosque was occupied and by August that year, Wheeler's own officer, Shankar Das recorded the defacements he saw there:

…a number of stones inside Sher Shah's Mosque at Purana Qila have been broken by the refugees intentionally. Out of this damaged lot unique pieces of carved marble in the Mihrab have been mutilated. Attempts were also made to rake out black

1.11 Gumbad Fateh Jang as it appears today. Photograph: Nayanjot Lahiri.

1.12 and 1.13 Refugees at Humayun's Tomb, Delhi. Courtesy ASI.

1.14 Sher Shah's Mosque at Purana Qila, Delhi. Courtesy ASI.

1.15 A view of the Purana Qila refugee camp. Courtesy ASI.

marble ornaments from the geometrical pattern incised in the splays adjoining the Mihrab. Some of the Refugees have started sleeping on the "Charpois" inside the Prayer Chamber and shoes are freely moved about.[9]

During his inspection, Das also found the prayer chamber of the mosque littered with bricks and pebbles, obviously used for causing injuries to the structure.

The Ministry of Relief and Rehabilitation was asked to take steps to prevent the mosque from being the victim of further acts of vandalism but no action appears to have been taken. In December 1949, another Survey officer, K.N. Puri, wrote to the chief commissioner about what he had observed there:

I was shocked to see some brick marks on the Central Mehrab of Sher Shah's Mosque. Brickbats were also seen piled at

one corner. Somebody appeared to have worked for its mutilation. Fortunately the bricks themselves being of war quality could not achieve the purpose for which they were used, as the injuries inflicted were not very serious. This was obviously the task of school children who could not administer sound blows to the marble ornamentation. The school was on and the students as well as the teachers were moving in the mosque with shoes on. Chairs were found spread up both in the Lawn and the outer court. It is a pity that in spite of various letters having been issued to responsible quarters due sympathy and cooperation should not have been invoked to save this gem in the history of Indian Architecture.[10]

Many other historic monuments were similarly defaced and these episodes, in retrospect, compel us to recognize that, for all practical purposes, protected monuments that had become refugee camps were not in the ASI's custody. Under these circumstances, all the Survey could do was to inspect monuments and prepare notes of strong protest—which it did—about how its suggestions were being completely disregarded by those in charge of relief and rehabilitation. Unfortunately, since the primary intention of the Ministry of Relief and Rehabilitation was to accommodate as many refugees as possible with no concern at all for the historic surroundings that housed them, the damage caused to some of the monuments was appalling.

Such incidents, unsurprisingly, attracted adverse publicity. Enquiries about various Muslim shrines were regularly made by the Pakistan government. On many occasions, photographs appeared to show how the Indian government was treating its Islamic monuments. Ruined gardens, gaps in fortifications made for egress and ingress of refugees, soot-blackened tombs, bulldozer operations levelling mounds that contained the foundations of old habitations inside monument compounds—these figure frequently in the letters and memos of the ASI, and surely they must have figured in media reports as well.

By the early 1950s, as refugees moved out, as always, it was the ASI, the institutional guardian of protected monuments, that immediately got down to the business of repairing and restoring them. Such repairs were carried out with commendable speed and so thoroughly that hardly anyone who visits those monuments today is aware of the tribulations and travails undergone by them more than six decades ago. The rusted incidents recounted here have simply been relegated to the dustheap of forgotten files in the archives of the Survey.

Partitioning the ASI, Museums and Archaeological Collections

Like other government departments at independence, the ASI was partitioned, along with its staff and assets. The Partition Secretariat as

early as July 1947 had suggested that departments were to proceed immediately in making arrangements for the transfer of officers and staff "at present located on the wrong side of the new borders to the areas they have elected to serve".[11] In the case of the ASI, some of these arrangements were in place, with the ASI officer Q.M. Moneer having been appointed as Director of Archaeology of Pakistan. Moneer in early August was already anxious about carrying equipment to Pakistan to set up his office there. On his request that he should be provided with photographic materials, chemicals, drawing and survey instruments, he was informed there were no reserves to spare in Delhi but such material was likely to be in stock with the Frontier Circle of the ASI (which would soon be part of Pakistan).[12] Instead, he was given a list of the stationery that could be spared for the requirements of his office for one month, ranging from scissors and gum brushes to shorthand notebooks and typewriters (figure 1.16). Clearly, the relocation of ASI equipment and staff was, at this point of time,

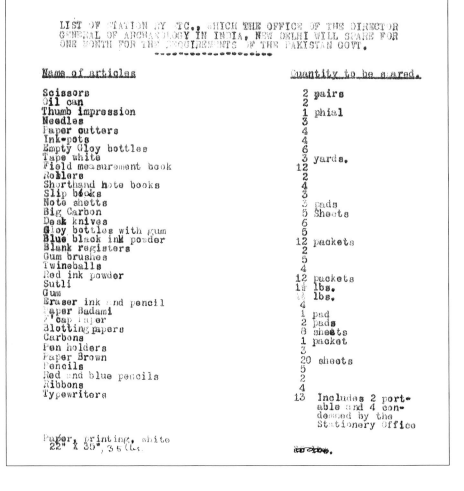

seen as only a minor blip that would blow over within a month after independence.

The arrangements, though, did not work according to plan. Following independence and partition, many employees who had opted to relocate to India or to Pakistan remained stranded on the wrong sides of the border for unanticipated stretches. They ranged from support staff to senior officers. Kala Singh and Sundar Das who were chaukidars at Harappa, and Musa, a sweeper in the Mohenjodaro Museum, had elected for India, but even months after independence they were still in Pakistan. The bulk of the staff of what would become the Department of Archaeology in Pakistan—including Q.M. Moneer, Director of Archaeology (Pakistan)—were stuck with their families in a refugee camp in Delhi till early September. Their journey to Pakistan, in fact, required the intervention of the ASI's Director General. In a letter to the Chief Administrative Officer, Pakistan (based in Delhi), Wheeler wrote on September 12, 1947:

1.16 List of stationery that was given for a period of one month to the ASI (Pakistan) from ASI (India). Courtesy ASI.

1.17 A pot from the Harappan period in the collection of the National Museum, New Delhi. Photograph: Nayanjot Lahiri.

1.18 A section of the collection from Harappa and Mohenjodaro, in the National Museum, New Delhi. Photograph: Nayanjot Lahiri.

In Purana Qila at the present moment, is an organized party [which] is a majority of the staff of the Pakistan Department of Archaeology, which has been recruited from the personnel of my own Department. Its director is Mr. Q.M. Moneer, and I enclose a nominal roll.

I am informed by your Headquarters that this Department is destined for Lahore, and my petition is that, if you can, without gross unfairness to others, do anything to assist them to reach their destination, you would be helping a particularly worthy group of recruits to Pakistan. They are of course in no worse plight than many others, but, as their former Chief, I naturally have a strong predilection in their favour and would most earnestly commend their present unhappy case to you.[13]

If facilitating the movement of staff from one country to another was difficult enough, much more complicated was the partitioning of antiquities and museum collections on both sides of the border.[14] On the face of it, this could have been a fairly straightforward exercise since the division could be done either by sharing the antiquities or on the basis of where the sites were located. As things turned out, in searching for a solution that was equitable to both nations, the negotiations became prolonged and convoluted. The Partition Council in October 1947 had resolved that museums would be divided on a territorial basis, while exhibits of the museums in provinces that were partitioned would be physically split. On this basis, the exhibits in the Lahore Museum, which had belonged to the United Province of Punjab before partition, were to be split between East Punjab (in India) and West Punjab (in Pakistan). This was straightforward enough.

More complicated was the fate of objects that had been sent on temporary loan to places that, on August 15, 1947, happened to be on the wrong side of the border. In its wisdom, the Partition Council ruled that all objects that had been removed for temporary display after January 1, 1947 were to be returned to the original museums. Because of this, there was a real problem regarding the antiquities of Mohenjodaro since as many as 12,000 objects from there were in Delhi on the day of partition. Since Mohenjodaro fell within the territory of Pakistan, the objects should have fallen to its share. However, India's negotiators maintained that these rightfully belonged to India because they had not been removed after January 1, 1947 from the original museum (which was at Mohenjodaro) but had come from Lahore. Additionally, they had not been removed for temporary display but because, as early as 1944, the Director General of Archaeology, Mortimer Wheeler, had wanted to concentrate all the best Indus objects in a Central National Museum.

It was this—the question of the intention about the future disposal of the objects in a Central National Museum in Delhi—that was key to the dispute around how the antiquities were to be divided. Several formulas were suggested and rejected, and pressure tactics were used by both parties. In order to make things difficult, the West Punjab government postponed the actual handing over of East Punjab's share of the Lahore Museum holdings till such time as India had handed over to Pakistan its share from the proposed central museum. And a final decision on the setting up of the National Museum remained pending till the Mohenjodaro matter was sorted out.

Eventually, after many rounds of negotiation and a massive exchange of correspondence, the Museum Committee in 1949 agreed to a division down the middle. More than 14,000 antiquities from the Indus sites were divided in this way, ranging from seals and statuary to more common artefacts of clay, stone and metal. That is how the National Museum in New Delhi came to own its superb collection of antiquities from the Harappan cities of Pakistan (figures 1.17 and 1.18).

The suggestion to divide the Indus collections into equal parts was made by Mortimer Wheeler who, after completing his term as Director General of Archaeology in India, had become the Government of Pakistan's

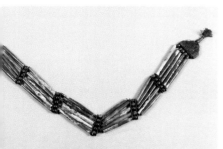

1.19 Part of the Mohenjodaro girdle with carnelian and bronze beads. Courtesy National Museum, New Delhi, Acc. No. 49.244/104.

1.20 Part of the Mohenjodaro necklace with beads of gold, agate and jasper. Courtesy National Museum, New Delhi, Acc. No. 49.244/105.

archaeological advisor. Wheeler suggested a similar formula for dealing with unique articles that could be divided, as for instance, jewellery made up of beads and spacers. Here, too, he suggested absolute equity. That this suggestion was accepted and foisted unthinkingly on several objects (with the division being eventually done by Wheeler himself) was tragic in retrospect. The partitioned objects included two gold necklaces from Taxila, Mohenjodaro's famous carnelian and copper girdle, and a magnificent necklace, also from Mohenjodaro, made up of jade beads, gold discs and semiprecious stones (figures 1.19 and 1.20). These and other antiquities were fragmented "equitably" by an archaeologist who, above all, should have known that he was severely compromising their integrity.

Situations like this surely raise a larger issue about the desirability of equity as the overriding principle for dividing museum collections and antiquities. In the case of India and Pakistan, the destruction of the integrity of monuments had been an important area of concern since the latter part of the 19th century, and it is somewhat amazing that such concerns were now forgotten when museum collections were partitioned. This is especially surprising since in February 1947 itself, the relics and relic caskets of two of the Buddha's disciples that had been taken away (presumably) from Sanchi to England in the 19th century began their journey back, eventually reaching Sanchi in 1952. Evidently, in the case of collections that were the subject of dispute, archaeologists and negotiators, in their anxiety to adhere to what was politic, ignored the more ethical option. In the bargain, the past came to be partitioned in this unfortunate way.

Notes

1 Nayanjot Lahiri and Sanjukta Datta, "A Past Lost & Changed", *8th Day—The Sunday Statesman Magazine*, Calcutta edition, June 19, 2005.

2 Nayanjot Lahiri, "Delhi: Memorializing 1857", in Nayanjot Lahiri, *Marshalling the Past: Ancient India and its Modern Histories*, Ranikhet: Permanent Black, 2012, p. 130.

3 H. Bullock, *Short History of the British Monuments and Graves Section*, Office of the High Commissioner for the United Kingdom, British Monuments and Graves Section (Head: Monuments [Historical]), London: Oriental and India Office Collection, 1951.

4 Ibid.

5 Iqbal Qaiser, *Historical Sikh Shrines in Pakistan*, Lahore: Punjabi Historical Board, 1998, pp. 66, 76 and 94.

6 For details and references relating to the fate of these Islamic monuments, see Nayanjot Lahiri, "Partitioning the Past: India's Archaeological Heritage after Independence", in Geoffrey Scarre and Robin Coningham (eds.), *Appropriating the Past: Philosophical Perspectives on the Practice of Archaeology*, Cambridge: Cambridge University Press, 2013, pp. 295–311.

7 Shankar Das, Confidential Note, File No. 14L/2/48. Report on (the monuments of) Alwar and Bharatpur. New Delhi: ASI, 1947.

8 Mortimer Wheeler, Letter to Relief and Rehabilitation Commissioner, dated April 10, 1948. File No. 15B/3/48. New Delhi: ASI, 1948.

9 Shankar Das, Note to D.G.A., dated August 25, 1948. File No. 15B/8/48 (Protection of Humayun's Tomb and Pir Ghaib occupied by Refugees). New Delhi: ASI, 1948.

10 K.N. Puri, Letter to Chief Commissioner of Rehabilitation, dated December 8, 1949 (Occupation of archaeological monuments in Delhi by refugees). New Delhi: ASI, 1949.

11 H.H. Patel and Mohammad Ali, Letter to Deputy Secretary Education Department, dated July 11, 1947. File No. 2G/19/47 (Staff of the Director of Archaeology Pakistan). New Delhi: ASI, 1947.

12 Q.M. Moneer, Letter to D.G.A., dated August 11, 1947. File No. 2G/19/47, ibid.

13 Mortimer Wheeler, Letter to Chief Administrative Officer Pakistan, dated September 12, 1947. File No. 26/23/47. New Delhi: ASI, 1947.

14 The references to files pertaining to the partitioning of museums are available in Lahiri, "Partitioning the Past".

2 Institution Building and Archaeological Research

The impact of independence and partition on monuments and museums is one element in the trajectory of India's archaeological heritage since 1947. The other element, examined here, is that of institution building and field investigations. The institutional framework relating to India's post-independence archaeological heritage, as this chapter will show, was not strikingly different from what had been put in place by the first half of the 20th century, as the existing structure was consolidated and expanded rather than replaced. Independent India's institutions and those of the pre-independence British Raj, in fact, are helix-like, in that you cannot discuss one without also drawing attention to the other. The priorities and scope of archaeological investigations undertaken in the years following independence, on the other hand, emerged out of independence and the partitioning of the country. At the same time, as this chapter highlights, important new research paths were opened up that appear to be unrelated to those political developments.

Since Jawaharlal Nehru's prime ministerial years anchor the direction along which independent India initially moved (figure 2.1), it is broadly around those years—from 1947 till the mid-1960s—that this first phase of rebuilding, research and expansion is analysed here.

Understanding the Institutional Framework

Institutionally speaking, 1947 was not a watershed year for Indian archaeology. For one, India's heritage policy remained very similar to that of the British Raj. The Ancient Monuments and Archaeological Sites and Remains Act of 1958 was the successor to the relevant acts of British India; if anything it was even more strongly weighted in favour of the union government ("union" and "central" are used interchangeably by me) than previous ones. Whereas the Act of 1904 had conferred wide powers upon collectors, these now came to be substantially transferred to the Director General of the Archaeological Survey of India. For another, the changes that can be observed post-1947 had actually started some years before independence. They began in the early 1940s as a consequence of a 1938 report penned by the British archaeologist, Leonard Woolley.

Woolley had come to India on the invitation of the Indian government. There was, by then, a real sense of the deleterious consequences of the government policies relating to archaeology that had followed Britain's financial crisis of 1931. The ASI had reached an unusually low ebb. Archaeological work was not being carried out through any sustained policy and nor were defects in technical training of personnel being addressed. The personnel pool itself had shrunk because of a retrenchment policy as a consequence of which the ASI had been surgically and unwisely pared. In the junior grades, for instance, the organization was so inadequately staffed that no trained succession to the senior posts could be guaranteed—there were a mere three junior officers as against 11 senior posts that were expected to be filled in the early 1940s. Woolley's report dealt with all this, and with many other issues. Crucially, Woolley urged the government to appoint for a limited term a Director General or Advisor who had the necessary experience but was not directly or indirectly part of the ASI. Accepting his advice, the British archaeologist Robert Eric Mortimer Wheeler was appointed. Wheeler arrived in India in April 1944. It was he who would oversee the partitioning of the ASI in 1947, as described in chapter 1 (figure 2.2).

On being appointed, Wheeler immediately got the government to approve the first

2.1 Prime Minister Jawaharlal Nehru at an exhibition organized by the ASI. S.R. Rao, the excavator of Lothal, is explaining the character of a ceramic display to him. Courtesy ASI.

2.2 Mortimer Wheeler during a visit to India after his tenure as DG, coinciding with the centenary celebrations of the ASI in 1961. Courtesy ASI.

2.3 A meeting of the Central Advisory Board of Archaeology in the 1970s, with the Education Minister Nurul Hasan in the chair, M.N. Deshpande (DG ASI) to his right, B.K. Thapar to the right of Deshpande, followed by Professor H.D. Sankalia of Deccan College (Pune). Courtesy ASI.

major recommendations for strengthening the ASI, and this was followed by proposals in 1945 to the Standing Committee of the Indian Legislature on Education which recommended that immediate steps be taken to give effect to its reorganization. Wheeler also included proposals in his recommendations that extended beyond the ASI—from integrating archaeological research and teaching into the universities to the creation of a Central National Museum in India for art, archaeology and anthropology. So, the changes that were carried forward well into the first years of independence had their genesis in the course correction that began in 1944. By 1947, these had begun to yield results.

What was the nature of the reorganization that had taken place prior to 1947? Deficiencies in staff had started to be addressed. The training of this staff had also been taken in hand. Two schools for training in archaeological techniques of excavation and documentation—one in Taxila in the north, and the other in Arikamedu in the south of India—had been opened. Apart from the ASI staff, these schools were attended by students and staff from Indian universities,

from museums and from the archaeological departments of the princely states. The Central Advisory Board of Archaeology was formed with the idea of getting scholars and institutions outside the ASI to offer advice on archaeological matters.

Simultaneously, Wheeler in 1945 laid out a roadmap for furthering the technical standards of Indian archaeology. Broadly, three main points were emphasized: one, to ensure constant contact between the ASI and similar institutions in Asia, Europe and America, and between the ASI and the Indian universities; two, to encourage Indian universities to establish training in archaeology and incorporate aspects of archaeology in the general curriculum "on the grounds that a reasoned appreciation of India's cultural heritage should form a normal part of a liberal education"; three, to bring specialized archaeologists from abroad for limited periods of time for the training of Indian workers and to send selected ASI officers on deputation to Europe and America to enlarge their experiences through exposure to the nature of work being done there.[1] The most striking aspect of the reforms introduced by

2.4 Sisupalgarh excavation team photograph. B.B. Lal is seated on the right of Amalananda Ghosh—both wearing ties. Courtesy ASI.

2.5 Prime Minister Nehru's note of April 7, 1959, after visiting the excavations being conducted by the Allahabad University in Kausambi. Sourced from G.R. Sharma, *The Excavations at Kausambi (1957–59)*, Allahabad: University of Allahabad, 1960. Courtesy Department of Ancient Indian History and Archaeology, University of Allahabad.

Wheeler were aimed at expanding the scope of archaeology from the confines of a government department into an instrument of the highest educational value.

Independent India's institutional framework for archaeology was rooted in these sentiments and changes. The Central Advisory Board of Archaeology which had been established some years earlier continued to function as a national board (it still meets annually) (figure 2.3). The idea of a Central National Museum was accepted in 1947, and its nucleus became the collection that had formed the exhibition of Indian art and archaeology held in London in 1947–48. When that exhibition returned home, it came to be displayed for the public in Government House (now Rashtrapati Bhavan). Although this exhibition was closed after some time, and some of the loaned objects were withdrawn by the respective owners, the government decided to use the remaining core collection to set up a permanent museum.[2] With government support, the National Museum was inaugurated on August 15, 1949 in New Delhi. The collection remained temporarily in Government House, and only in December 1960 moved to the building on Janpath, specially made to house its collection.

Archaeological training under the aegis of the ASI also continued. In 1948, B.B. Lal, a young officer of the ASI who had been schooled by Wheeler in Taxila, organized a training school for archaeology at Sisupalgarh in Orissa (figure 2.4). Some 40 research students from various Indian universities and institutions as also from China and Sri Lanka participated. The excavation there was conducted according to the principles laid down by Wheeler and revealed a substantial early historic fortified city about which more will be said a little later. Within a decade, in 1959, the "School of Archaeology" in the ASI was founded (upgraded in 1985 to an "Institute of Archaeology"). This was meant to provide training to those in service as well as to postgraduate students admitted in its programme from India and neighbouring countries.

It was also in 1958–59 that the teaching of archaeology in academia received government support. This happened when the University Grants Commission (UGC) decided to start departments of "Ancient Indian History and Archaeology" in half a dozen universities. This

Last December I visited the Kausambhi museum at the University. I was pleased and a little surprised to see a noteworthy collection. Today I visited the Kausambhi site about which I had heard a great deal for many years but which I had never visited previously.

It was evident even from a rapid view that this is a site of great importance from the historical and archaeological points of view. Also that the work being done there is methodical and expert. I am glad that the Allahabad University is in charge of it and I congratulate it —

Jawaharlal Nehru
April 27th 1959

is not to say that prior to this there was no archaeological teaching and research at universities. In Calcutta University, some archaeology-related courses had been introduced in the early part of the 20th century, while the Asutosh Museum of Indian Art of the University began excavations at Bangarh in 1937. Again, Kausambi began to be excavated by Allahabad University in 1948 (figure 2.5) and Baroda by the Maharaja Sayajirao University there in the early 1950s. At the same time, by creating separate university departments with a specific focus on archaeology, the government aimed to signal that the academic mainstreaming of archaeology through central funding, which Wheeler had strongly emphasized, had commenced. It is another matter that, since the initial push, archaeology departments in universities have not been seeded with the same urgency.

The formation of state departments of archaeology was the third conspicuous move that was undertaken from the 1950s onwards. The Department of Archaeology and Museums in Rajasthan was started in 1950 while the State Department of Archaeology of Uttar Pradesh was established in 1951. There were, though,

a few hiccups along the way. The UP State Department, for instance, lost its independent status in 1953 when the responsibility of its work was transferred to the State Museum, and it was only in 1958–59 that it regained its former status. The pace was not the same everywhere. In Orissa, while the Orissa Ancient Monuments Preservation Act was passed in 1956, the Department of Archaeology was only established in 1965 and that too as a subordinate office, functioning under the Department of Tourism and Culture. In the case of Maharashtra, while with the states' reorganization in 1960 the Maharashtra Government Department of Archives and Historical Monuments was given charge of monuments other than national ones, it was only as late as 1970 that the Department was renamed the Department of Archives and Archaeology. In other states, the genesis of a regional department existed in the form of the work done by erstwhile princely states. So, while the Kerala State Department of Archaeology evolved in its present form in 1959, this was as a consequence of the integration of the Departments of Archaeology in the erstwhile states of Cochin and Travancore. Some of the state departments, it should be mentioned, soon went on to publish reports on the sites they excavated in their respective states. These included Utnur by the Directorate of Archaeology of Andhra Pradesh, and Kaundinyapura jointly by the Education and Social Welfare Department and the Department of Archaeology of Maharashtra.[3] This was not the case with all states; the Department of Archaeology and Museums in Rajasthan, till date, has not published a single comprehensive report of the sites it has excavated.

Archaeological Research

What about the larger research priorities of archaeological studies in the immediate post-independence phase? There were continuities and changes. The two problems that had been identified by Mortimer Wheeler while planning for archaeological research in 1944–47 remained crucial. These related to the large gaps in the sequence of cultures that constituted the protohistory and early history of India. In the north, it was the gap of a millennium or more between the end of the Indus civilization and the advent of the Achaemenid empire in the 6th century BCE, which was problematic. As far as south India was concerned, the problem was more wide-ranging since the basic proto-historic and historical configuration prior to the Greco-Roman phase of interaction (c. 1st century CE) itself was unclear. From 1945 until 1947, a timetable of south Indian cultures came to be built up with a sequence made up of a stone axe culture, megalithic and local Andhra levels, along with the stratigraphic presence of pottery that had Mediterranean designs. Such pottery was found at Arikamedu in Pondicherry and at Brahmagiri in Karnataka.

Post-independence, in north India, two excavations directed by the ASI partially filled the cultural gap to which Wheeler had earlier pointed. These were at Ropar in Punjab and at Hastinapur in Uttar Pradesh (figures 2.6–2.8). In both instances, the sequences that were unearthed embodied timelines that stretched from protohistory till the medieval period. Y.D. Sharma's excavation at Ropar showed that the first settlers there were Harappan, and after a long desertion, the site was reoccupied by people using Painted Grey Ware (PGW, an Iron Age culture of the early 1st millennium BCE). Hastinapur's base culture was different—an Ochre Coloured Pottery (OCP) which was, as in the case of Ropar, followed by the PGW phase, and then by a long sequence of cultures till the medieval centuries.[4]

Elsewhere too, the ASI took up work within the parameters of the research problems that Wheeler had outlined. B.B. Lal's excavations at Sisupalgarh in Orissa, for instance, aimed to look for ceramic markers of the kind that were found at Arikamedu and Brahmagiri by Wheeler, and Lal must, no doubt, have felt elated that rouletted ware of what was described as being of Roman inspiration was found there. Wheeler's shadow over the excavations went beyond the search for a Roman connection. The digging

was done according to the Wheeler method— where a trench was laid across the fortifications, where a gateway was excavated, and where an interior area was taken up to understand the cultural sequence (figures 2.9 and 2.10).[5] It is a pity, though, that this fortified city site was excavated for only one season, with the sole purpose of ascertaining its cultural sequence and chronology. The reason for this remains unclear since the excavator himself noted that at least three or four field-seasons were necessary at Sisupalgarh to bring to light a "reasonably good picture of it".[6]

2.6 Ropar—view of the excavated mound. Courtesy ASI.

2.7 Ropar—mound and surveyor at work. Courtesy ASI.

2.8 Hastinapur—view of the main mound. Courtesy ASI.

2.9 Sisupalgarh gateway. Courtesy ASI.

2.10 Sisupalgarh—view of the gateways flanking the street. Courtesy ASI.

India's archaeological history was being fleshed out through field research undertaken by other institutions as well. A major achievement of the first decade after independence, in fact, was the body of research that revealed a steady occupation in different parts of India by a variety of cultures and people. Some of this work was done by universities, especially the Deccan College, Poona and the M.S. University, Baroda. The range of sites that these universities focused on were largely concentrated in central India and the Deccan—Nasik, Maheshwar, Navdatoli and Nevasa are some of them. Baroda, which was beyond this geographical segment, was also excavated. The cultural evolution exposed through these excavations, in many instances, spanned several millennia. Nasik's sequence on the banks of the Godavari stretched from the 1st millennium BCE to the 19th century, while that of Maheshwar on the northern bank of the Narmada was pushed back to the late Stone Age, followed by chalcolithic and historical phases. At Nevasa on the banks of the Pravara river, the six cultural periods were even more impressively long— from the lower palaeolithic till what used to be called the "Muslim-Maratha" phase (with a large chunk of time when there was no habitation, from the 4th till the 14th century CE).

One aspect that needs to be remembered about this research is that while the end result was the successful building up of the archaeological foundations of ancient India in a way that mitigated the idea of a gap in the cultural development of India, in several cases an important motivating factor was the idea of providing an archaeological basis for India's religious texts. B.B. Lal's work at Hastinapur and at several other sites in north India is an instance in point where attempts were made to link the material culture with the Aryans and the *Mahabharata*. This is evident from Lal's own writings where he noted that "there is circumstantial evidence to associate the Painted Grey Ware industry with the Aryans". He also believed that since many of the sites where PGW was found—Hastinapur, Ahichchhatra,

Kampila, Tilpat, Bagpat etc.—were associated with the story of the *Mahabharata*, it would seem that the Ware was associated with early settlers "who formed part of the Aryan stock in India".[7] Similar is the case with the Deccan College work at Maheshwar. H.D. Sankalia, in his memoir *Born for Archaeology*, mentioned that when he was quite young, he had heard that Maheshwar was ruled by King Sahasrarjuna of the Haihayas, which had hugely impressed him since Sahasrarjuna "alone among all the kings had defeated Ravana".[8] But, after commencing excavations, Lal soon realized that instead of material remnants of the times of a Puranic king, it was a chalcolithic nucleated agricultural settlement of the 2nd millennium BCE which had emerged out of the mounds.

If it was archaeologists who carried forward the fieldwork required to fill in the gaps in the evolution of protohistoric and early historic cultures in different parts of north and south India, the decision to take up the search for Harappan sites was proactively pushed by India's leaders. As early as March 1948, K.M. Panikkar—a scholar administrator who had just finished serving as the Diwan (minister) of the princely state of Bikaner—had written to Prime Minister Nehru about the necessity for a survey of Bikaner and Jaisalmer. This was based on what had been conveyed to him by the archaeologist Aurel Stein:

> With the separation of the Pakistan Provinces, the main sites of what was known as the Indus Valley Civilisation have gone to Pakistan. It is clearly of the utmost importance that archaeological work in connection with this early period of Indian history must be continued in India. A preliminary examination has shown that the centre of the early civilization was not Sind or the Indus valley but the desert area in Bikaner and Jaisalmer through which the ancient river Saraswati flowed into the Gulf of Kutch at one time.[9]

Nehru promptly agreed with the suggestion which was conveyed to the Survey, and with his support, money was also allocated for it.

Consequently, in 1950, Amalananda Ghosh of the ASI began an exploration in Bikaner. Within a couple of months he unearthed as many as 70 sites, 25 of which yielded the same types of antiquities that had been found at Harappa and Mohenjodaro. The sites extended across a wide area, from the Pakistan border up to midway between Hanumangarh and Suratgarh in the Sarasvati valley, and about 24 kilometres east of Bhadra near the border between Bikaner and Punjab. Kalibangan was one of them, which was described by Ghosh as "the eastern-most outpost of this culture"[10] (the ASI being unaware that Harappan seals had been found there more than 30 years before, by Luigi Pio Tessitori in 1917–18). Excavations began at Kalibangan in 1960–61 and continued for nine seasons until 1968–69 (figures 2.11–2.13).

2.11–2.13 Kalibangan—views of street, well and fire "altars" on the citadel. Courtesy ASI.

30   MONUMENTS MATTER

Soon enough, the ASI made the search for Harappan sites within the national borders of India a national project—to be carried forward by Indian archaeologists. The Swedish archaeologist Hanna Rydh, known for her excavations at the historical site of Rangmahal in Bikaner, had initially wanted to dig a Harappan site in that area but, after the initial parleys, was told that Indian archaeologists who had made discoveries there ought to be the first to conduct such an excavation.[11] This, it is relevant to mention, is no longer the case. A part of the excavations at Rakhigarhi, the largest Harappan city in India, was financed by the California-based Global Heritage Fund. This began before the ASI's own excavator had submitted his report on the excavations that he had earlier conducted there.

A few years after the Harappan discoveries in Bikaner, as was earlier mentioned, Ropar came to be excavated between 1953 and 1955. The discovery of an Indus seal among other objects there established the northward extension of the Harappan culture. For the Harappan civilization's extension south and southeast of Sindh and Rajasthan, the ASI undertook work in large parts of the Bombay State (now in Gujarat). S.R. Rao directed much of this work. Extensive explorations were combined with intensive excavations at a few sites. Between 1953 and 1958, the village-to-village survey of the region revealed the wide dispersal of sites of the Harappan tradition all across this stretch. In Saurashtra itself, some 40 Harappan sites were discovered. Two key places, Rangpur and Lothal, were excavated. Dug between 1953 and 1958, Rangpur revealed the penetration of the Harappan civilization into the Kathiawar peninsula, its survival in a "decadent" form till the end of the 2nd millennium BCE, and a continuous cultural sequence there which stretched from 2000 to circa 800 BCE. The Lothal excavations (from 1954 till 1963) uncovered a small, impressively planned township where key features associated with the Harappan civilization that had been uncovered in Sindh and Punjab—such as city planning marked by

excellent streets and drains, workshops for the production of beads and metal objects, and the presence of inscribed Harappan seals—now emerged in Gujarat. What were new here were the elaborate dockyard and warehouse that were evidently related to an elaborate infrastructure supporting a maritime trade that included the Persian Gulf and beyond (figures 2.14 and 2.15).

The decade after independence, thus, saw a dramatic closing of the gap between protohistoric and early historic India. There were Harappan sites in the north and west, and a plethora of other cultures—some contemporary with the Harappan and others following its demise—in areas across western and central India as also in the Deccan. Simultaneously, archaeologists involved in these field programmes were actively exploring interactions among these cultures and the overlaps between them. There was actually a subcommittee made up of ASI officers and university excavators who in 1958, after carefully examining the material, came to a consensus on the similarities in ceramics among these sites. The work of this subcommittee was discussed by B. Subbarao in his 1958 edition of *The Personality of India*, where he also clearly articulated the

2.14 Lothal—large basin (dockyard). Sourced from *Indus Civilization Sites in India: New Discoveries*, ed. Dilip K. Chakrabarti, Mumbai: Marg, 2004. Photograph: DPA/Milind A. Ketkar.

2.15 Vice-President Zakir Hussain visiting Lothal. S.R. Rao is behind him. Courtesy Nehru Memorial Museum & Library.

impressive evidence of overlap and interlocking cultures. Subbarao pointed out, on the one hand, the presence of post-Harappan cultures with phases of those which were derived from the Harappan, and on the other, the presence of chalcolithic people, with local variations in culture, up to the borders of Mysore, but in contact with each other.[12] The implications of commonalities and overlaps were subsequently taken further by S.R. Rao who clearly saw the links, as he put it, "between the late and post-Harappan cultures of Gujarat and the central Indian chalcolithic cultures" which, as he underlined, explained how some of the Harappan traditions survived and became part of later chalcolithic cultures.[13]

Thus, not only was the Harappan civilization showcased, through post-independence research, as having deep roots in India, it was simultaneously shown as having become part of a larger cultural milieu which survived the civilization's demise.

Monument Protection and Development

I will end this chapter by coming back to the political calls that were taken at the highest levels of government in relation to the archaeological universe of post-independence India. While the proactive state push which resulted in the discovery of Harappan sites in India has already been discussed, there are a couple of other key developments that are also worth remembering.

One significant initiative concerned conservation practices. Today, the idea of creating a protective zone around monuments is part of the legal framework that aims to protect archaeological sites. The idea itself, that a security net ought to be created around heritage buildings, can be traced back to Jawaharlal Nehru. As Prime Minister, he is known to have complained to the Union Minister of Education in 1955 that India's old and historical places were getting spoilt by new buildings being put up around them. In order to protect them from such intrusions, Nehru suggested that the government "lay down that within a certain area no building should be put up without permission".

An example of his proactive approach on creating such protective barriers is the enclosure encircling the tomb of Abdur Rahim Khan-i-Khana in Nizamuddin. This was built after Nehru had visited the site and suggested that the adjacent grounds be converted into a small garden because, as he put it, he did not want Nizamuddin Extension East to extend into the area around the tomb. This idea eventually found its way into the Ancient Monuments and Archaeological Sites and Remains Rules of 1959 which unambiguously, for the first time, noted a prohibited and a regulated zone around protected sites and monuments.

What, though, of situations where protecting sites and monuments conflicted with economic development? This question became a key one in the 1950s where plans for building a massive irrigation dam across the Krishna river were drawn up. A major implication of these plans was that once the dam became functional, the large number of structures that made up ancient Nagarjunakonda would be permanently drowned in the river waters (figure 2.16). Nehru's confidential note on the subject to Maulana Azad, the Education Minister, emphasized the dilemma and what he believed had to be done. He wrote:

2.16 A view of Nagarjunakonda before the construction of the Nagarjuna Sagar dam. Courtesy ASI.

68246

2.17–2.19 Relocated remains of a mahachaitya, a vihara (Site 43) and an apsidal temple enshrining a Buddha image (Site 4) at Nagarjunakonda. Photographs: Upinder Singh.

This morning I performed the ceremony of laying the foundation-stone of the great dam of Nagarjuna Sagar…. Afterwards, I went to the site of the excavations of the ancient cities of Sri Parvat and Vijayapuri. Nearly all this vast area is going to be submerged when the dam is built and which will be called the Nagarjuna Sagar. This site of excavations is one of the most important and vital in India. The idea that this place, where so much of our ancient history and culture lie hidden under the earth, should be lost forever under the new lake has distressed me greatly. Yet the choice had to be made for the sake of the needs of today and tomorrow.[14]

In order to save as much as was possible, the ASI was tasked with a massive project of exploration, excavation and documentation. Consequently, before the valley was turned into a gigantic lake, about 136 new structures and structural complexes were unearthed; nine of the most important structures were transplanted and rebuilt on top of the Nagarjunakonda hill and on the banks of the reservoir (figures 2.17–2.19); smaller-scale replicas of 14 other structures were also made.

In these early years of independence, in the face-off between development and conserving precious heritage, India's commitment to development overrode the need to protect the integrity of monuments. This is a path, as later chapters will reveal, from which the country has not diverted.

Notes

1 R.E. Mortimer Wheeler, "The Archaeological Survey of India: Note on Its Present Reconstruction, 1945". File No. 28/5/45 (Standing Committee of the Indian Legislature on Education). New Delhi: ASI, 1945.

2 J.K. Roy, "The National Museum of India", *Ancient India* 9, 1953, pp. 246–49.

3 F.R. Allchin, *Utnur Excavations*, Hyderabad: Government of Andhra Pradesh, 1961; M.G. Dikshit, *Excavations at Kaundinyapura*, Bombay: Director of Archives and Archaeology Maharashtra State, 1968.

4 For an overview of this work, see B.B. Lal, "Protohistoric Investigation", *Ancient India* 9, 1953.

5 For scope of the work and a summary of the results, see B.B. Lal, "Sisupalgarh 1948: An Early Historical Fort in Eastern India", *Ancient India* 5, 1949, p. 67.

6 Ibid.

7 Lal, "Protohistoric Investigation", pp. 93 and 97.

8 H.D. Sankalia, *Born for Archaeology: An Autobiography*, Delhi: B.R. Publishing Corporation, 1977, p. 62.

9 K.M. Panikkar, Note to the Prime Minister, dated March 29, 1948. File No. 19/8/48. New Delhi: ASI, 1948.

10 An early description of the Rajasthan discoveries is available in A. Ghosh, "The Rajputana Desert: Its Archaeological Aspect", *Bulletin of National Institute of Sciences of India* 1, 1952, pp. 37–42.

11 Elisabeth Arwill-Nordbladh, "Decolonising Practices? Some Reflections Based on the Swedish Archaeological Expedition to Rajasthan in India 1952–54", in Ola Wolfhechel Jensen (ed.), *Histories of Archaeological Practices: Reflections on Methods, Strategies and Social Organization in Past Fieldwork*, Stockholm: The National Historical Museum, 2012, pp. 281–82.

12 Bendapudi Subbarao, *The Personality of India: Pre- and Proto-Historic Foundation of India and Pakistan*, Baroda: M.S. University, 1958 edition, pp. 153–54. The work of the subcommittee is also mentioned by Subbarao here.

13 S.R. Rao, "Excavation at Rangpur and Other Explorations in Gujarat", *Ancient India* 18 and 19, 1962 and 1963, p. 19.

14 This note of December 10, 1955 has been cited by Upinder Singh in "Buddhism, Archaeology and the Nation: Nagarjunakonda 1926–2006", in Nayanjot Lahiri and Upinder Singh (eds.), *Buddhism in Asia: Revival and Reinvention*, New Delhi: Manohar, 2015, p. 149.

Prehistoric India and Its Changing Frontiers

3

So far we have explored the fate of monuments and archaeology from the perspective of the impact of political developments as also in relation to institution building and research in the first 15-odd years after independence. This chapter, and the two that follow, look at archaeological discoveries and research in India from the 1960s till the present. These are examined in relation to a very large chunk of time, stretching from prehistory, across protohistorical cultures till the historical period.

The cumulative research in all its wealth of detail is available in books, reports and articles.[1] While this research can be presented with any degree of magnification, given the character of this volume it is neither possible nor suitable to offer a comprehensive assessment of research in the last five or six decades. Instead, a compressed broad-brush picture is presented which provides a sense of the expansion of the archaeological database, some of the important achievements in various domains and regions, as also glimpses of new methods and areas of research. Simultaneously, the many challenges and problems that hamper an in-depth understanding of the archaeological history of India as a whole will also be considered.

How "Ancient" is Ancient India?

A first question that is crucial is how ancient are the earliest traces of humans in India. Unless one knows how far the presence of our prehistoric ancestors can be pushed back, the ubiquitous stone tools that turn up practically all over India (figures 3.1 and 3.2) are reduced to being markers for which there is no firm chronology.

While the search for the trail of early humans in India goes back to the 19th century, it is the last 30 years or so that have yielded early scientific dates from geological contexts bearing prehistoric stone artefacts. Unlike Africa, Europe and parts of Asia, no early hominid fossil finds have been located in South Asia. An unequivocal discovery was the cranial vault found in 1982 at Hathnora village near Hoshangabad (Madhya Pradesh) and, subsequently, a collarbone. These, though, appear to belong to a 24–35-year-old woman of an archaic *Homo sapiens* category, and are not of the same antiquity as are hominid finds from many parts of Africa and Asia.

If hominid finds are few and far between, what we do have is an impressively early prehistoric presence in the form of artefacts. First, in the Indian Siwalik range (figures 3.3–3.5), in situ artefacts were found in a geological context called the "Pinjor zone of Upper Siwalik formation". This is dated to more than 1.8 million years ago. In the Upper Siwaliks, there are early palaeolithic artefacts from Uttarbaini (Jammu), and these are likely to be 2 million years old.[2] This matches what was discovered

3.1 and 3.2 Palaeolithic stone tools (left) and microliths (right) from Manesar in Gurgaon, Haryana. Photographs: Nayanjot Lahiri.

3.3 Stone tools from the Siwaliks. Photograph: Parth R. Chauhan.

3.4 and 3.5 Views of the Indian Siwaliks. Photographs: Parth R. Chauhan.

about the dates of prehistoric horizons in Riwat and the Pabbi hills of Pakistan. The second area from where there is an impressively early chronology is Tamil Nadu, from the site of Attirampakkam (figures 3.6–3.8).[3] On the basis of techniques like palaeomagnetic dating and cosmic ray exposure dating (applied for the first time in India), our prehistoric ancestors there have been shown to be present between 1.07 and 1.5 million years ago, using hand axes and cleavers that are generally designated as "Acheulian". This makes Attirampakkam the oldest Acheulian site in India. There is an equal possibility of early dates in other parts of India like Karnataka and Maharashtra. So, the answer to how ancient is ancient India would be fairly straightforward. It is some 2 million years old.

The other element which archaeological research since independence has built upon is a body of evidence about the environmental changes that took place even as early South Asians first went about their daily lives. An appreciation of this has largely emerged through research on what are described as natural archives: marine sediments (from ocean floor), fluvial sediments (transported by water), aeolian sediments (transported by wind), lacustrine (lake) and peat deposits, ice cores and tree rings.[4] In many instances, these contain markers of environmental changes on a macro-scale. Marine sediments from the Bay of Bengal and the Arabian Sea, for example, have been carefully studied to help reconstruct shifts in the pattern of monsoon winds over the last several thousands of years. Warmer surface-dwelling species in the marine cores reveal a weak southwest monsoon some 21,500 years ago while its strength seems to have increased in two steps at 15,300–14,700 and 11,500–10,800 years ago, as the increase in deeper-dwelling species reveals.[5] Tectonic action involved in the creation of mountains had an effect on surrounding regions and impacted hominids in a variety of ways. For instance, from research done in the last 40 years or so, it has become evident that about 2 million years ago, the Tibetan plateau was slightly higher than the Himalaya; that the formation of Nanga Parbat, one of the highest peaks of the Karakorum, is largely the product of the last million years; and that the 1900-metre-high Salt range immediately south of the Potwar is no less recent.[6]

Catastrophes beyond the Indian subcontinent have also been shown to have had an undeniable impact here. The Indonesian Toba volcanic super-eruption of 74,000 years ago is

3.9 Toba ash seen at Jwalapuram in the Jurreru valley. Photograph: Ravi Korisettar.

an example of this, whose ash has been identified in different parts of India. In the Kukdi basin near Pune, the ash bed varies between 20 centimetres and 1 metre, over a length of about 3.5 kilometres.[7] Interestingly, gravel lenses underlying and overlying the ash bed contain palaeolithic tools and this has also been observed in the Jurreru valley of Andhra (figure 3.9). While one can only imagine the darkness that set in as a consequence of ash-laden clouds, and what its likely impact on the lifeways of various prehistoric communities was, the presence of similar tools prior to and after the Toba eruption means that in these parts of India, the settling ash did not wipe out human existence.

Palaeolithic Arenas of Activities

As we move from a few million to a few hundred thousand years ago, the data accumulated from archaeological investigations over the last 70 years become more thick and widely spread. The problem in India, it is necessary to remember, has never been that of scarcity of evidence of palaeolithic sites. The abundance of palaeoliths was well understood by the late 19th century itself—from practically all parts of India where there is suitable raw material— as were many of the stratigraphic contexts in

which they occurred. What was lacking was a firm chronology, and more recent research has helped to somewhat mitigate this by producing more reliable dates. So, for instance, we know that Acheulian occurrences which in the case of Attirampakkam were very early, are also to be found in Umrethi (Gujarat) a little over 190,000 years ago; in the Hungsi valley (Karnataka) 174,000–166,000 years ago; and in the Son valley (Madhya Pradesh) 140,000–110,000 years ago. Absolute geochronological techniques for dating the middle and upper palaeolithic assemblages of many significant sites have been employed as well, and the results in those instances also underline long chronologies for those phases of prehistory.

Importantly, they highlight the coexistence of different types of occurrences. For instance, in coastal Saurashtra (Gujarat), there are middle palaeolithic occurrences that date to around 35,000 years ago which is about the time period when a more specialized tool kit, characteristic of the upper palaeolithic assemblage, occurs in Jwalapuram (Andhra Pradesh). This, incidentally, is true for later cultural phases as well. In the Ganga plains, as recent research has revealed, around 8000 and 6000 years ago, when mesolithic hunter-gatherers lived around meander lakes and streams, an early agricultural society existed at Lahuradeva in the Ganga alluvium. Post-independence research, thus, reveals that it is not a stagewise evolution that unfolds across India, with one type of culture replacing another. On the contrary, prehistoric India can now be seen as a pastiche of various coexisting adaptations.

Archaeological sites are generally disturbed and much more so in the case of palaeolithic arenas of activity. That makes the discovery of primary sites or places where people actually lived or manufactured stone tools or discarded them, extremely important. The number of primary sites, in relation to the total occurrences in an area, is not large. One exception is the cluster of 11 such sites that were found in the Hungsi valley of Karnataka, some of which were the camps of hunter-gatherers.[8] Their distribution shows a deliberate choice of the valley area. In the valley, almost all of them lie close to the banks of streams. In some instances, granite blocks have been moved by the occupants perhaps to serve as windbreaks. Many primary prehistoric habitation places were also found in Madhya Pradesh—in rock shelters and as open-air sites. Bhimbetka in the Raisen area, excavated from 1972 onwards, is marked by several rock shelters that were used for habitation and for manufacturing Acheulian tools. Beyond rock shelters, in the Raisen area itself, relatively undisturbed open-air palaeolithic sites, more than 90 of them, were also found in the 1960s and '70s.[9]

Only rarely do sites of this type yield relict remains of possible habitation structures. An exception is Paisra in the Munger district of Bihar where in the 1980s, a palaeolithic working-cum-habitation locality yielded multiple postholes. While these would have originally held timber poles that have since disintegrated, the evidence is "distinctly suggestive of thatched superstructures of a temporary nature" and this is the first evidence of its kind in India.[10] In another part of the same site, deliberately created stone alignments, one of which is in association with a posthole, also suggest the construction of another kind of structure there.

A third type of palaeolithic site is that of Baghor I in Madhya Pradesh, where fascinating evidence beyond that of stone tools and their manufacturing was found.[11] On the one hand, a hearth was excavated which must have been used for cooking. On the other hand, there is the first shrine platform ever discovered in India. Circular in form, in the centre of this platform several fragments were found which, when joined together, formed a triangular natural stone with laminated coloured concentric triangles. While it is unknown what this signified to the inhabitants of Baghor I, it is similar to the stones that are worshipped as emblems of the goddess or mai (mother) by local people there even today.

"Hunter-gatherers" is how the people who inhabited these archaeological sites would be described, but the question of how specific data pertaining to their subsistence patterns are recovered also needs to be considered. There is a singular absence of plant remains and animal bones which show signs of being the waste remnants of human meals. In many instances, the nature of the stone assemblage has been of help in underlining the possible uses of different tools and artefacts for hunting and gathering. Hand axes at Yediyapur in the Hungsi valley of Karnataka would have been used for butchering animals and extracting marrow. Stone crushers, according to the excavator, were probably used for pounding plant foods like seeds, grains, nuts, berries and tubers.[12]

An exciting way of recovering data on subsistence is microwear analysis, which studies the use-wear polishes on stone artefacts. An example of this is the 1980s study of the lithic assemblage from Baghor III, not far from Baghor I which was earlier described.[13] Of the 47 artefacts with use-wear, 26 (55.3 per cent) appear to have been used on plant or wood and 21 (44.6 per cent) on meat, bone, antler or hide. Among the 59 bladelets, 52 (88.1 per cent) were used on plant or wood—such as rattan palm, bamboo, grasses and the banyan tree—while the remaining, merely seven specimens, had been used on "non-vegetal materials" like meat, bone, antler and hide. That this is not unique to Baghor III emerges from a similar analysis done of an assemblage of artefacts from the Dhanuhi rock shelter, an upper palaeolithic site in the Rewa district of Madhya Pradesh (figures 3.10–3.14), which demonstrate the various kinds of polish that have been recovered through microwear analysis.[14] Here too, the shaped tools were used more frequently on "vegetative than on non-vegetative materials". The pattern, thus, that emerges at these sites is of a diet of various vegetable foods and fruits, which may well mean that these are gatherer societies in which animal meat did not have an overwhelming dietary presence.

How have archaeologists in India reconstructed ways of thought and religious practices in palaeolithic times? The evidence that

(anti-clockwise from top left)
3.10 Dhanuhi—boring-scraping antler polish. Photograph: Prakash Sinha.

3.11 Dhanuhi—boring-scraping palm-type polish. Photograph: Prakash Sinha.

3.12 Dhanuhi—boring-scraping bamboo-type polish. Photograph: Prakash Sinha.

3.13 Dhanuhi—cutting grass-type polish. Photograph: Prakash Sinha.

3.14 Dhanuhi—cutting meat bone-type polish. Photograph: Prakash Sinha.

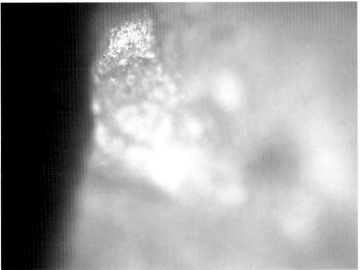

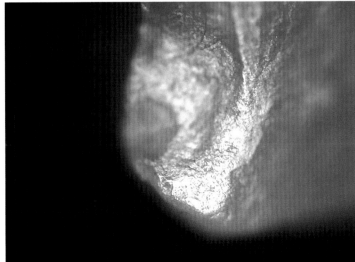

has been unearthed is not extensive but shows the importance of the female principle. Baghor I, as earlier mentioned, is dramatic with its ritual placement of a laminated stone on a deliberately constructed platform. That the lamination resembles a female vulva was pointed out by the excavators, and the importance of the female principle is further underlined by a figurine find at Lohanda Nala in the Belan-Son area.[15] Here, a piece of bone that had been fashioned into a female form is suggestive of the antiquity of cults around "goddess" figurines in palaeolithic central India.

Cognitive belief is also writ large in Bhimbetka.[16] There, the rock shelter III F-24 leads through a 25-metre-long tunnel to a hall where there is a large rock with a flat vertical wall with deep cupules (figure 3.15), and close by on a boulder is a well-shaped circular mark with an adjacent meandering groove line. Similar evidence—of engraved lines and cupules—was recovered from Daraki-Chattan in the Chambal basin. These are believed to indicate some kind of symbolic belief. Additionally, ostrich eggshell beads have been found at many places including Patne, Bhimbetka and Khaparkheda. Some objects were embellished with designs. Patne yielded an ostrich eggshell with parallel lines and cross-hatching on it, while a fluted stone core from Chandravati in Rajasthan was engraved with a rhomboid design.

Practically all of this, from carvings and engravings to the fascinating manifestations of the female principle, has emerged out of post-independence research, and one hopes that in the future, more such data will flesh out the image of a palaeolithic India that is more than a mass of minutiae about stone tools and their typology.

Mesolithic Hunter-Gatherers

Beyond the "Old Stone Age", the important research around more advanced societies of hunter-gatherers is worth mentioning. These are generally described as mesolithic cultures and several hundred such sites have been discovered across large parts of India. These were cultures that used microliths (generally stone tools between less than 1 to 5 cm in length), and the appellation of mesolithic for these groups is an allusion to their temporal position in the "Middle Stone Age" between the palaeolithic hunter-gatherers and the neolithic ("New Stone Age") marked by the advent of food production. Stone is the most common material used for manufacturing tools, although at Damdama in the Ganga plains, antler, bone and horn tools are used. Microwear analysis of microliths from the Vindhyas and the Ganga plains has been done and this reveals that they were used for scraping, sawing, cutting, drilling, incising and grooving while the tentative contact materials were likely to have been hide, meat, soft plants, grass, reeds, wood, bones and antlers.[17]

Thanks to a number of excavations and surveys, advanced hunter-gatherer societies have been shown to occupy various ecological

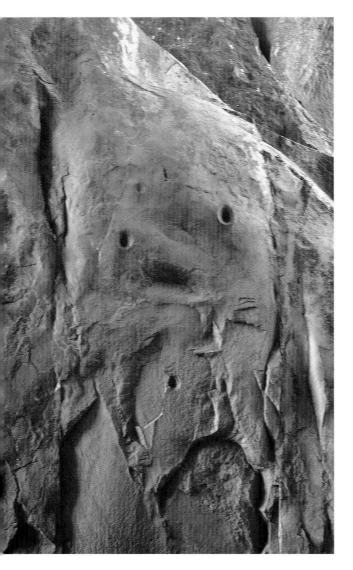

3.15 Bhimbetka—view of cupules. Photograph: Nayanjot Lahiri.

settings—including those that were seldom exploited by palaeolithic cultures. The sites in the central Gangetic plains of UP are examples of this, many of which are clustered around horseshoe lakes or marshy depressions known locally as tals. It is around these that specialized mesolithic clusters are found—especially in the Allahabad–Banaras zone. Some are small, marked by only a handful of microliths. There are other sites that are larger, such as Damdama, Mahadaha and Sarai Nahar Rai which have provided extensive evidence of a deep-rooted mesolithic occupation on the central Ganga alluvium.

The dates that are now available on mesolithic sites reveal that their beginnings go back to a time period of circa 26,000–23,000 BCE at places like Batadomba-Lena in Sri Lanka and Patne in Maharashtra. This would make the earliest mesolithic societies contemporaries of upper palaeolithic hunter-gatherers. After the advent of the Holocene around 10,000 BCE, food-producing societies began to emerge in different areas of the Indian subcontinent and, as research has revealed, several mesolithic sites seem to have coexisted and interacted with such agriculturists. A few millennia after this, mesolithic societies disappeared although microliths as a tool category continued to be occasionally present.

These were foragers with a difference. For one, post-independence research has shown that in several instances, along with hunting and gathering, domesticated animals were occasionally used and cultivated food consumed. The faunal assemblage at Bagor in Rajasthan shows wild cattle, deer, river-turtle, pigs and rats.[18] Alongside, domesticated goat and sheep also figure prominently, and some domesticated cattle. The inclusion of agricultural foodstuffs in the hunter-gatherer diet can be inferred in a number of ways. In the case of Langhnaj in Gujarat which was likely to have been a contemporary of the Harappan tradition, this is underlined by skeletal remains that show the resident population as having very bad teeth. This is attributed to the period of

inclusion of agricultural foodstuffs in the hunter-gatherer diet. On an average, mesolithic sites in South Asia show an incidence of dental caries of around 4.8 per cent while here it was 8 per cent. It is entirely possible that the foodgrains/cereals were obtained from a neighbouring group of agriculturists.

Evidence of coexistence and interaction, in turn, raises a number of issues. A question that needs to be considered is why, despite access to farming ways of life, such mesolithic groups did not embrace the animal husbandry and agricultural practices of their near neighbours. Why did they continue with their foraging strategies? Was it because these strategies were extremely successful and, consequently, there were no pressures to move to a different kind of subsistence regime? Again, if mesolithic hunter-gatherers had access to cattle with domestic ancestry, as the archaeological records show, did they treat them as domesticates? There is a difference between domestic and domesticated and, in a situation of coexisting societies, one is not completely sure if there was animal-rearing by mesolithic people or whether they treated these animals, which may have come from agro-pastoral groups, in the same way as they treated those that were hunted.

What is certain is that in particular contexts, mesolithic sites were not temporary camp sites but settlements that were continuously inhabited. The data on sedentism as an aspect of the Uttar Pradesh mesolithic sites are worth emphasizing. Site occupation was around oxbow lakes and streams issuing from them, and that it was year-round is indicated by the teeth of hog deer and swamp deer from the faunal assemblages at Mahadaha and Damdama:

> The ages at which wear commences for different molars of hog deer and swamp deer are roughly known and they indicate a wide range of killing seasons. For example, taking April and July as the months of birth of hog deer and swamp deer respectively, the unworn and slightly worn lower permanent molars indicate a wide range of months for human occupation at

Mahadaha. But even if we confine the analysis to fully erupted but unworn teeth, then the mere presence of such lower molars of hog deer indicates August (M1), April (M2) and December (M3) as the periods of occupation at Mahadaha. Likewise, July and January are indicated by the molars of swamp deer.[19]

Because the inhabitants could so reliably work out their food supply, regular residential mesolithic sites have been found in this region. This is indicated by the relatively thick and continuous occupational deposits at some of them; at Mahadaha, the four layers constitute a 60-centimetre-thick deposit while at Damdama the nine layers are even more impressive, with a thickness of 1.5 metres. Other evidence of sedentary settlements occurs not only in the form of hut floors, pits for storing grain and human burials, but also heavily utilized querns and mullers, and even bandicoot remains that suggest all-round occupation at the site. Semi-sedentary sites have also been excavated in the northern Vindhyas where cultural remains include hut floors, postholes suggesting covered structures, grinding stones indicating processing of plant food, storage bins and a great deal else.[20]

That this kind of residential permanence may have created a more complex society than what is generally attributed to hunting-gathering communities has also emerged from post-independence research. The general burial practice was that of extended burials in shallow, oblong graves that are found within the habitation area, frequently close to hearths. Such contextual associations as the presence of refuse material from the hearths indicate that the dead were intentionally buried with elements that evoked life, in this case fire and its transformative aspects. Incidentally, the Ganga valley sites are not the only ones which have provided evidence of mortuary practices. On the southern edge of the Ganga plains, along the northern Vindhyas, Lekhahia—a site marked by rock shelters and open-air occurrences—has yielded skeletons. Again, Bagor in Rajasthan is marked by burials with grave goods. What makes the situation of the Ganga plains sites distinctive is the sheer scale of evidence where about 80 graves were found in the habitation areas of three sites.

Biological information that has been extracted from mesolithic human skeletal remains can now tell us about diet, work and pathology.[21] In the skeleton of a young woman from Baghai Khor, porotic hyperostosis was noticed, which can be caused because of nutritional stress or infectious diseases. At Sarai Nahar Rai, dental caries rates are low, which underlines a relatively high-protein and low-carbohydrate hunting-foraging diet. On the other hand, the anterior and posterior permanent teeth are large, an adaptive trait in a lifeway demanding not merely masticating of tough food but the use of the mouth for holding objects or sharpening and breaking down fibrous materials.

Finally, there is now a profusion of information about rock art associated with mesolithic India. Rock shelters with paintings of mesolithic times have been extensively documented across large parts of Madhya Pradesh and the hilly southern edge of Uttar Pradesh. It is worth emphasizing that this is, almost entirely, a post-independence development even though, in many instances, such paintings were present in the vicinity of monuments

3.16 Sanchi—view of paintings in a rock shelter. Photograph: Nayanjot Lahiri.

that were documented from the 19th century onwards. Sanchi exemplifies this, where "rock paintings but a few steps away from the stupas of Sanchi—not to speak of the numerous and well-preserved paintings seven hundred metres away on Nagauri hill—went unnoticed and unmentioned" during the long period when the excavation and restoration of its Buddhist monuments was underway (figure 3.16).[22]

What appears striking is how rock art can be integrated with other evidence. Take, for instance, the presence of rhinoceros bones at various mesolithic sites in the Ganga plains. While the question of whether the animal was hunted and its meat consumed has been a subject of controversy among archaeologists, the paintings from the northern Vindhyas clearly underline that hunters attacking the rhino was a very common depiction, with one representation that shows butchering of the animal.

Attempts to date this art have largely depended upon the subject matter of the paintings on the walls and ceilings of the shelters themselves (figures 3.17–3.19). This is not entirely satisfactory since it ignores the possibility of individual styles continuing over long periods of time as also the overlaps that exist between different phases. Some of the paintings have been scientifically dated. However, the largest number of paintings are in red haematite, and datable carbon can only be obtained from the white gypsum-bassanite paintings. The dates from this paint suggest a range between 5200 and 1100 years ago, and thus the absolute dates do not seem to be early.[23] Microerosion dating—which looks at the ages of fractures on crystals caused at the time of the production of petroglyphs—done on cupules at Morajhari and Moda Bhata in Rajasthan has provided an earlier chronology, between 10,000 and 5000 years ago.[24] Obtaining many more precise dates for the profusion of prehistoric rock art in India should be tackled on a priority basis by scholars working in this field.

This perhaps points to the core challenge that faces the study of prehistoric India. While

knowledge about it has expanded in many impressive ways due to new and major discoveries, this needs to be matched with equally intensive offsite research. Advances in our knowledge depend as much on such research as on archaeological excavations and explorations. If there are large caches of prehistoric tools found in sites around different parts of India, there must be, at the very least, half a dozen such sites in each of those regions where microwear analysis is done on these tools. If India has a rich and continuous prehistoric record, the urgency of comprehensively generating associated scientific dates for this record needs to be realized—which requires many more laboratories where chronometric dating on archaeological samples is regularly done. The state of affairs is exemplified by the fact that the Archaeological Survey of India, the premier government body conducting archaeology in India, has not published any scientific analysis of value concerning

3.17 Bhimbetka—"auditorium" rock shelter. Photograph: Nayanjot Lahiri.

3.18 Bhimbetka—painted animals on the wall of a rock shelter. Photograph: Nayanjot Lahiri.

prehistory in the last few years. Again, if the prehistory of a great extent of north and west India is reasonably known, the same cannot be said for northeast India where large parts of the landscape are a total blank. If these issues are seriously tackled, many more breakthroughs are likely to be made in the future.

Notes

1 For references to books and articles, see the publications of Dilip K. Chakrabarti, especially *India: An Archaeological History* (second edition), New Delhi: Oxford University Press, 2009 and *The Oxford Companion to Indian Archaeology: The Archaeological Foundations of Ancient India*, New Delhi: Oxford University Press, 2006.

2 For a summary of discoveries in India and Pakistan, see Chakrabarti, *India: An Archaeological History*, pp. 51–53. For an excellent overview of the palaeolithic record of the Indian subcontinent, see Parth C. Chauhan, "Stratigraphy, Typology and Technology of the Palaeolithic Record", in Dilip K. Chakrabarti and Makkhan Lal (eds.), *History of Ancient India Vol. I: Prehistoric Roots*, New Delhi: Vivekananda International Foundation and Aryan Books International, 2014, pp. 67–120.

3 Shanti Pappu, Yanni Gunnell, Kumar Akhilesh, Regis Braucher, Mauric Taieb, Francois Demory

and Nicholas Thouveny, "Early Pleistocene Presence of Acheulian Hominins in South India", *Science* 331, 2011.

4 Ashok K. Singhvi and Vishwas S. Kale, *Palaeoclimate Studies in India: Last Ice Age to the Present*, New Delhi: Indian National Science Academy, 2009, p. 3.

5 Ibid., p. 14.

6 For changing environments in the northwest, see Bridget Allchin, "Early Human Cultures and Environments in the Northern Punjab, Pakistan: An Overview of the Potwar Project of the British Archaeological Mission to Pakistan (1981–1991)", in Statira Wadia, Ravi Korisettar and Vishwas S. Kale (eds.), *Quaternary Environments and Geoarchaeology of India*, Bangalore: Geological Society of India, 1995, pp. 153 ff.

7 Subhrangsu Kanta Acharyya and Prabir Kumar Basu, "Toba Ash on the Indian Subcontinent and Its Implications for the Correlation of Late Pleistocene Alluvium", *Quaternary Research* 40, 1993, pp. 10–19. Also, see R. Korisettar, T.R. Venkatesan, S. Misra, S.N. Rajaguru, B.L.K. Somayajulu, S.K. Tandon, V.D. Gogte, R.K. Ganjoo and V.S. Kale, "Discovery of a Tephra Bed in the Quaternary Alluvial Sediments of Pune District (Maharashtra), Peninsular India", *Current Science* 58, 1989, pp. 564–67.

8 K. Paddayya, "The Acheulian Culture of the Hungsi Valley, South India: Settlement and Sub-

3.19 Bhimbetka—painted boar. Photograph: Nayanjot Lahiri.

sistence Patterns", in V.N. Misra and Peter Bellwood (eds.), *Recent Advances in Indo-Pacific Prehistory*, New Delhi: Oxford & IBH Publishing Co., 1985, pp. 59–64.

9 Jerome Jacobson, "Acheulian Surface Sites in Central India", in ibid., pp. 49–57.

10 P.C. Pant and Vidula Jayaswal, *Paisra: The Stone Age Settlement of Bihar*, Delhi: Agam Kala Prakashan, 1991, p. 48.

11 J.N. Pal, "Baghor I", in Chakrabarti and Lal, *History of Ancient India Vol. I*, pp. 372–81.

12 K. Paddayya, "Yediyapur", in ibid., p. 509.

13 Prakash Sinha, "Economic and Subsistence Activities at Baghor III, India: A Microwear Study", in Jonathan Mark Kenoyer (ed.), *Old Problems and New Perspectives in the Archaeology of South Asia*, Wisconsin: Department of Anthropology, University of Wisconsin, 1989, pp. 47–53.

14 Prakash Sinha, "Cogitating Prehistoric Archaeological Landscape with Pattern Recognition", conference on *Computer Applications to Archaeology*, Williamsburg, VA, 2009.

15 R.K. Varma, V.D. Misra and J.N Pal, "Madhya Pradesh and Adjoining Uttar Pradesh: Palaeolithic Cultures of the Belan and Son Valleys", in Chakrabarti and Lal, *History of Ancient India Vol. I*, p. 159.

16 All references to rock art here and to objects with decoration are from Giriraj Kumar, "Rock Art", in ibid., pp. 312–19.

17 J.N. Pal, "Microlithic Industries and the Issue of the Mesolithic", in ibid., p. 278.

18 For a summary of the evidence from Bagor and other mesolithic sites, see Chakrabarti, *India: An Archaeological History*, pp. 100–10.

19 Umesh Chattopadhyaya, "Settlement Pattern and the Spatial Organization of Subsistence and Mortuary Practices in the Mesolithic Ganges Valley, North-Central India", *World Archaeology* 27(3), 1996, p. 468.

20 Pal, "Microlithic Industries and the Issue of the Mesolithic", pp. 262–63.

21 The data on biological anthropology of human skeleton remains have been summarized in V.N. Misra, "Mesolithic Culture in India: Keynote", in V.D. Misra and J.N. Pal (eds.), *Mesolithic India*, Allahabad: Department of Ancient History, Culture & Archaeology, University of Allahabad, 2002.

22 Erwin Neumayer, *Prehistoric Indian Rock Paintings*, New Delhi: Oxford University Press, 1983, p. 1.

23 G. Kumar, R.G. Bednarik, A. Watchman and R.G. Roberts. "The EIP Project in 2005: A Progress Report", *Purakala* 14–15, 2005, pp. 13–68.

24 Kumar, "Rock Art", p. 310.

4 Redefining the World of Protohistoric India

From the spectrum of hunting-gathering cultures, we turn to the expansion in our understanding of the range and depth of protohistoric societies. "Protohistory" has been used in India for describing a large chunk of time that begins with the advent of food production and ends with the beginning of early historic India. There is a range of societies that flourished in this phase, across 7000 years or so—from the 8th millennium BCE when farming makes its presence felt in Baluchistan, till the 1st millennium BCE which marks the advent of the historical period in India. This chronological and geographical depth has largely emerged out of the field research done in different parts of the Indian subcontinent since 1947. Consequently, the term "protohistoric India" which earlier tended to conjure up images of India's first urban culture, the Indus or Harappan civilization, has now become an umbrella term that describes a wide range of societies that cover practically all of South Asia. There are the first food-producing societies that stretch from Baluchistan to the Gangetic plains; the Harappan civilization and its contemporary cultures; neolithic horizons in Kashmir and the peninsular south; pioneer farmers of Malwa, Maharashtra, Bihar and Bengal; and iron-using horizons in different parts of the Indian subcontinent.

While protohistory denotes a cultural phase where there may not have been writing in a particular region even while the region is mentioned in the written records of a literate contemporary group, the historical period begins with the presence of writing. In India, though, questions of terminology and periodization are more complex. So, for instance, India's first civilization, the Harappan civilization, is described as protohistoric even though it had a very elaborate system of writing, since this has

4.1 General view of Lahuradeva and its adjoining lake. Photograph: Rakesh Tiwari.

not been deciphered. As for the first presence of deciphered writing in India, it goes back to the 5th century BCE inscriptions on pottery in Tamil Nadu (discussed in the next chapter). At the same time, in north India, while knowledge of writing is likely to go back to the same time period since there are literary references to it, the archaeological presence of writing can only be firmly pushed back to Maurya times.

But coming back to the term "protohistoric", additionally, its usage for describing a plethora of cultures is considered appropriate because not only are these, generally speaking, chronologically prior to the historical period but also they are thought to foreshadow developments in historic India, from food patterns to artisanal and craft activities. Seeing the historical period as an outcome of some 7000 years of evolution and growth, however, is unsatisfactory in two different ways. First, it reduces the multiple protohistoric cultures of India which inhabited that large chunk of time to a kind of "supporting" role, a mere foundation or a series of stepping stones. It is unlikely that this is how the people of that time saw themselves and it is also not how we, from the perspective of the present, should see them and the regions they inhabited. Secondly, there are many aspects of historical India that are better understood in terms of the particular conjunction of circumstances that unfolded in the 1st millennium BCE. If this chapter has used the term "protohistoric", it is as a mere descriptive term—for the time period between the birth of food production and the beginning of history—and not one that is loaded with either of these connotations.

Beginning of Food Production

The beginning of farming in India is an area of research that has been marked by a virtual paradigm shift, one that began, if I recall, between 1976 and 1980. In 1976, I began my undergraduate education at St Stephen's College (University of Delhi). There, in the course on ancient India, the inception of farming used to be described as having occurred in West Asia from where it spread, through a process of

4.2 Lahuradeva—rice husk inclusions in pottery from Period IA. Photograph: Rakesh Tiwari.

4.3 Lahuradeva—rice grain impressions in pottery. Photograph: Rakesh Tiwari.

diffusion, to other parts of the Old World. One of the reasons for this was that till the 1970s, none of the early food-producing societies discovered in India and Pakistan provided scientific dates. The paradigm shift, when it happened, was sudden and dramatic. This followed the landmark excavations in 1977 at Mehrgarh in Baluchistan where a very early farming culture based on wheat and barley cultivation was discovered.[1] The first levels there, which belong to the 8th millennium BCE, show the presence of domestic wheat as also wild and domestic barley. The occurrence of local wild barley in the area of the Bolan pass suggested that it was independently domesticated here. Again, the proto-domestication and domestication of local wild goat, sheep and cattle were recorded from this level. The necessity of moving beyond a West Asian diffusionary hypothesis for understanding the advent of agriculture in India, thus, was first accepted due to the discoveries made at Mehrgarh.

The importance of Mehrgarh in underlining the presence of early farming is now complemented by an equally significant discovery in the heart of Gangetic India. This relates to an early centre of rice domestication at Lahuradeva in Uttar Pradesh (figures 4.1–4.3).[2] Excavated between 2001–02 and 2005–06, Lahuradeva has yielded wild and domesticated rice going back to the 7th millennium BCE. Additionally, the use of rice husk as a tempering material in making pottery underlines its abundant presence there. This was a community that cultivated rice and, additionally, gathered a number of wild plants. Apart from these discoveries, excavations at Jhusi in Uttar Pradesh and Bagor in Rajasthan have revealed that agriculture also seems to have been prevalent there in the 6th millennium BCE, and there is the possibility of early agricultural traditions elsewhere as well.

Taken together, what has emerged from Baluchistan to the Ganga plains suggests that the advent of food production in India was not a single event but a multi-strand tapestry.

Neolithic Horizons and Chalcolithic Cultures

Because of a growing body of research, one now encounters a range of food-producing societies a little later, from the 4th–3rd millennium BCE onwards, in a vast geographical swathe, from peninsular India to Kashmir. What is worth emphasizing is that the time lag between the birth of such cultures and the developments from Baluchistan to the Gangetic plains just described, does not necessarily mean that these later societies came up as a consequence of the migration of people or diffusion of food-producing traits from the earlier cultural horizons. Research on the southern neolithic ("ash mound") tradition makes this amply evident.

The southern neolithic is a 3rd millennium/early 2nd millennium BCE horizon. Geographically speaking, a large number of settlements have been located on the southern Deccan plateau, often associated with ash mounds derived from the burnt accumulations of cattle dung at sites of ancient cattle pens. What is striking is that its agricultural regime is qualitatively different from other subcontinental cultures of this time, and is logically the best adaptation in the lower rainfall area of south India. This is made up of small millets and tropical pulses like mung bean and horse gram, two species whose wild progenitors are known to occur in the region. Other non-indigenous species are also present but it appears that "native species were domesticated before the arrival of introduced species. It is, therefore, possible that south India represents a region of independent agricultural origins, albeit rather late by comparison to other world regions."[3]

In Kashmir, the settlements that have been excavated make it clear that we seem to be in the presence of people trying to cope with long, cold winters. They sought to mitigate the climatic rigours by living below ground level which is always warmer than the surface. The pit dwellings that they used as residences, along with the hearths that they lit to keep warm have been encountered at Gufkral and Burzahom.[4] Wheat, barley and lentils were cultivated while sheep, goats and cattle as also domestic fowl were kept. The bones of wild animals like ibex, deer, wolf and bear have been found as well, attesting to the fact that hunting continued to augment farming activities.

The large-scale presence of the first sedentary communities in other areas, however, has been shown to be chalcolithic—with copper and stone being simultaneously used. Rajasthan is an example of this where two distinctive cultures have been revealed—the Ganeshwar-Jodhpura culture in the northeastern part of the state and the Ahar culture towards the southeast. The early exploitation of copper is not surprising since both cultural zones are located in areas that are rich in copper mineralization. That the demand for copper of cultures antecedent to the Harappan civilization, from the Indus plains to Haryana, may have been one of the reasons for the burgeoning presence of copper-using sedentary food-producing societies in these segments of Rajasthan needs to be considered.[5] At least at Ganeshwar, the cultural sequence suggests that this was where copper objects (in Period II) were found in large quantities which bear similarities to those from Kalibangan. The arrowheads, rings, bangles, spearheads, chisels etc. go into several hundreds and could not have been manufactured only for the inhabitants of Ganeshwar which is a relatively small settlement. In the case of Rajasthan what also needs emphasis is that this phase is antedated by levels going back to the 5th millennium BCE which are described as "Mesolithic" (i.e. marked by microliths) that also seem to be distinguished by the presence of agriculture. So, the 4th millennium BCE chalcolithic traditions may well have emerged out of an earlier metal-free agricultural horizon.

These are all cultures that antedated the Harappan civilization. Prior to their discovery, it was fairly common to see that civilization as the supreme urban phenomenon whose demand for raw materials, for instance, facilitated the consolidation of regional cultures with which the Harappans had intimate interactions in various regions to the north, east and southeast. What has now become evident is that some cultures that had earlier been bracketed as contemporaries of the Harappan civilization have turned out to be much older and were, in fact, interacting with the early Harappans. Burzahom in Kashmir is an example of this, which yielded a wheel-made pot with 950 agate and carnelian beads whose provenance seems to be somewhere in the Indus plains, and another pot of the same type on which is painted the "horned deity" motif (also of Indus inspiration which occurs at Kot Diji in the Indus plains, in a context that antedates the Harappan civilization). So, even before the creation of Harappan cities, the neolithic and chalcolithic cultures of the northwest were not isolated cultural worlds.

The Harappan Civilization

It is more than 90 years since the discovery of the Indus civilization, now known also as the Harappan civilization, was announced by John Marshall on September 20, 1924 in *The Illustrated London News*.[6] Marshall's announcement inaugurated the first phase of research on the civilization, and since 1947 much has changed in the way in which it was originally perceived.

To begin with, there is its spectacular geographical spread. The Harappan civilization, in the first phase of research, was seen largely as a Sindh and West Punjab phenomenon with a marginal presence in Baluchistan and Gujarat. Today, we know that it included the deserts of Rajasthan in India and Cholistan in Pakistan, large parts of East Punjab (or Indian Punjab) and Haryana, parts of Uttar Pradesh and all parts of Gujarat, with even a trading post in Afghanistan. Shortughai in Afghanistan is entirely Harappan—with the archetypal pottery, seals, beads, even mud-bricks of the Harappan size. Shortughai perhaps represents the earliest Indian diaspora, a group of people who settled in a far-off land even while they maintained strong links with their homeland.

What was also foregrounded from the 1960s, with an acceleration from the 1970s onwards, is the presence of a long antecedent development of cultures that eventually transformed into the full-fledged Harappan civilization. Settlements practically all over the Harappan distribution area have revealed an abundance of such cultures with notable discoveries being made at Harappa, Kalibangan, Kot Diji, Dholavira, Bhirrana, Kunal and the large number of sites in Cholistan. The manner in which these cultures foreshadowed the appearance of the Harappan civilization is clear from the presence of various features in a few settlements: bricks in the classical Harappan ratio of 1:2:4, drainage and street systems, a variety of semiprecious stone beads, the manufacture of seals and weights, clear evidence of monumental construction and the appearance of some signs which later became part of the Indus script system. Many significant features of the classic civilizational phase of the Harappan tradition, thus, appear to have been present from the latter part of the 4th millennium BCE.[7]

Another aspect which is especially striking is that while in 1947, our ideas about the civilization were dominated by the cities of

4.4 Dholavira—view of a reservoir. Photograph: Nayanjot Lahiri.

Mohenjodaro and Harappa, today the picture is far more diverse. Apart from Mohenjodaro and Harappa, we can think of several other large urban centres. Among these are Gamweriwala in Cholistan which is spread over 81.5 hectares, Dholavira in Gujarat which is more than 100 hectares and Rakhigarhi in Haryana which is said to cover more than 300 hectares. Also, whereas earlier the cities were thought to be based on a uniform chessboard pattern, it is now clear that while there was centralized planning, the roads do not always move straight nor do they cross each other at right angles. Kalibangan's township is an example where, as the recently published excavation report puts it, "while the north–south thoroughfares were found to be unimpeded, the east–west running lanes or streets did not cut across the former and were staggered in plan".[8] Similarly, Dholavira is made up of three parts (the citadel divided into a "castle" and "bailey", the middle city and the lower city). Its other features, including remnants of stone pillar bases, a hoarding in the Harappan script, a large stadium-like area and hydraulic engineering of a very high order resulting in a series of reservoirs and dams, are also worth mentioning (figures 4.4 and 4.5).

There are also many types of settlements. Apart from the big cities, a second series of smaller centres have been revealed that recall the basic features and layout of the large centres, and below them very small urban settlements that were of commercial significance.

Among the smaller centres, Kalibangan (figure 4.6) has been shown to be like Mohenjodaro in that it had eastern and western segments, with the latter dominated by public structures including platforms with fire altars on them. What these settlements have revealed is also that there is no necessary relationship between the size of an urban centre and urban planning. Mohenjodaro may well have been 25 times

4.5 Dholavira—stadium in the foreground. Photograph: Nayanjot Lahiri.

4.6 Kalibangan mounds, with the modern pillars marking the edges of the protohistoric ploughed field found there. Photograph: Nayanjot Lahiri.

the size of Lothal. However, Lothal shares with it the careful planning of burnt-brick houses, and a well-laid-out alignment of drains and streets. In fact, it is the only town whose streets and lanes are uniformly paved with mud bricks and covered by a layer of kankar (lime). Finally, rural settlements have also occasionally been excavated, especially in Gujarat. What we know about them reveals that there were villages among them—Kanewal with a 1.5-metre-thick archaeological deposit had circular huts—as well as temporary semi-nomadic/nomadic sites. Nomadism has been shown to be an integral component of the world of Harappan India.

If our perspective on the civilization's urban centres has changed, so have our ideas of their food practices. Earlier, it was wheat and barley that were considered to be the standard cereals. Today, a much more diverse agricultural geography is what stands out, in which millet and rice were quite important. What is also worth underlining is that, apart from recovering plant remains through imprints on clay and through flotation, a beginning has been made in phytolith analysis and extraction of starch granules. At Farmana, starch granules were extracted from some 50 different surfaces including surfaces of pottery vessels, stone tools and dental calculus of human burials.[9] Starches belonging to barley and mango came from a variety of grinders and pounding stones, while traces of eggplant were recovered from the interior surface of storage jars. Ginger and turmeric starches were extracted from a cooking pot. Taken together, this has pushed back the antiquity of the use of ginger, turmeric and mango to Indus times.

On the question of cereals, significantly, rice occurs in many areas like Harappa in Punjab and Balu in Haryana which are not necessarily marked by a long tradition of rice cultivation. On the other hand, as we saw, domesticated rice has been shown to have a remarkably early presence in the Ganga plains, and it is entirely possible that knowledge of rice cultivation may have come from the east to the Harappan areas. The Harappan civilization, thus, no longer appears as a culture living in civilizational

autarky. Something as basic as its food was in important ways influenced by its contacts with contemporary cultures.

Along with agricultural societies, hunter-gatherers too were part of its contact zone. In fact, along with domesticated animals like cattle and goats/sheep, Harappans consumed various species of wild fauna for food. The ratio of wild animals in relation to domesticates is fairly high—approximately 1:4. How were wild animals procured? Were there hunters who were Harappan citizens or did they depend upon hunter-gatherers? Actually, it was probably both. The depictions of wild animals on seals, for instance, even of large ones like the elephant and rhinoceros, are very realistic and had to be based on an intimate knowledge of such animals. Alongside, as the case of Langhnaj (see chapter 3) reveals, there was a close interaction between Harappans and hunting-gathering societies.

Our understanding of Indus craft and trade has also evolved considerably. This has happened in a number of ways ranging from archaeological and scientific analysis to ethnographic and experimental insights. On the question of the application of science-based techniques, the breakdown of the chemical composition of Harappan copper and alloyed objects is an instance of how this has helped in the study of its craft traditions. From an analysis of data on the elemental composition of these artefacts in 1996, it has become evident that the tradition of working in copper of high purity dominated the Harappan tradition—of the 324 objects analysed till the 1990s, 184 were of pure copper. To put it another way, the Harappans were not primarily bronze-using people. As for ethnographic insights, these have been fairly successful in reconstructing the technical aspects of production—by observing indigenous craftspeople. For instance, in order to study the production of long-barrel cylinder carnelian beads in the Harappan context, the skills involved in making chasai beads in Khambat, also long-barrel like the Harappan specimens, were carefully observed.

The entire process, from knapping roughcuts to polishing the beads, required some seven years of apprenticeship. This possibly explains why the production of Harappan long-barrel carnelian beads remained in the hands of a very limited number of craftspeople.

Beyond the minutiae of manufacturing practices, the ways in which craft and trade depended on each other have emerged very strongly. One of the most striking features of craft production appears to be that it was not confined to areas where the raw materials were found. There were craft centres near sources of raw material, such as Nagwada and Nageshwar in Gujarat, manufacturing shell objects from sources close at hand. Interestingly, though, shell objects were also manufactured at places like Mohenjodaro which was fairly inland, far away from the coast that provided the shells. Evidently, this kind of craft could survive and prosper because of a well-organized system of trade. The Harappans obviously had the capacity to mobilize resources from various areas ranging from Rajasthan to Afghanistan—the discovery of Shortughai in Afghanistan which was likely to have played a role in the exploitation of lapis lazuli, tin and other raw materials substantiates this very well. At the same time, ordinary stone was also traded over long distances. The sandstone from Kaliana hills in the Bhiwani district of Haryana has been found at Harappan sites in Rajasthan and as far as Harappa in Pakistan Punjab. In much the same way, chert blades from the Rohri hills of Sindh reached Harappa on the one hand and possibly Lothal on the other.[10] Beyond such artefacts and raw materials, there are other exciting possibilities that need further investigation.

In this context, a brief analytical reconstruction of the difference in the state of knowledge on Harappan external trade from 1947 till the present is also desirable. By 1947, there was hard evidence that the Harappans had contacts and thus, by inference, trade relations with areas to the west and the northwest, mainly two—Mesopotamia and Iran. Today, there is evidence of contact with many more regions, and discoveries in Afghanistan, South Turkmenia and the Persian Gulf have expanded the frontiers of Indus trade. The inferences continue to be based on finds of objects that are indisputably of Indus origin or inspiration in those regions, as also Indus designs and motifs on their indigenous artefacts. Likewise, objects in India which are direct imports from regions to the west or are inspired by their craft and iconographic traditions form part of the expanding database. Finally, trade in various raw materials also features in the picture of civilizational contact. On the whole, though, while the Harappan civilization had varied contacts with cultures and civilizations in West and North Asia, in terms of quantum its subcontinental trade appears to have been far more impressive.

Cultures Contemporary with and Subsequent to the Harappan Civilization

The Harappan civilization did not exist in a cultural vacuum. On the contrary, important cultural configurations have emerged out of research on the peripheries of the Harappan distribution zone, and in other segments of inner India as well.[11]

Rajasthan, for instance, where many important Harappan settlements flourished, was also home to two other contemporaneous cultures. These are the later phases of the Ganeshwar-Jodhpura and Ahar chalcolithic cultures. What is worth noting in relation to what we know about the Ahar culture settlements of this phase is that we are not in the presence of an undifferentiated village culture. There are more than 80 sites, many of which are as small as a couple of acres (less than a hectare) while some occupy more than 10 acres (Ahar and Gilund would fall in this category). At some sites, several architectural features that appear to imitate the forms of contemporary Harappan towns have been uncovered. For one thing, Balatal is a fortified settlement with an area of about 500 square metres. Mud/mud-brick fortifications surround the two mounds of Gilund as well. Apparently, the smaller, higher eastern mound recalls the elevated areas of some Harappan sites while the western mound resembles the "lower town" of these sites.

Then, as we move towards inner India, various societies make their presence felt, in regions like the Malwa plateau, in Maharashtra and in the upper and middle Gangetic plains. The first chalcolithic farmers of Malwa, concentrated in the Chambal valley, are part of the Kayatha culture—the name of a place where this horizon was discovered post-independence. While the houses are unprepossessing, marked by mud and reed, 40,000 microbeads of steatite were found here which are identical to Harappan specimens. In the case of Maharashtra, the village society that is contemporary with the Harappans is the chalcolithic

Savalda culture, followed by a range of other cultures that continued well into the 1st millennium BCE. What is arguably the most carefully excavated chalcolithic site of Maharashtra is Inamgaon, whose voluminous report is an excellent window into what can be learnt about the remote past through a multidisciplinary excavation.[12] The study of soils there, for instance, found that the average nitrogen content in the sediments from houses is 0.031 per cent while the same in the soil samples from the courtyards is about 0.121 per cent, i.e. almost four times more than that present in the houses. This high nitrogen content was shown as being a sure indication that the courtyards were used for tethering domestic animals and for dumping animal waste.

Finally, as one moves north, a tapestry of village farming communities in Bihar and Uttar Pradesh has emerged. Chirand is an example of a fairly thick neolithic stratum (3.5 m) marked by a broad-based farming pattern. There are remains of crops like rice, wheat, barley and lentils while the animal remains include domesticated cattle and wild animals like elephant and rhinoceros. At the other end, in the doab area, the chalcolithic Ochre Coloured Pottery (OCP) culture shares the status of the first farming communities of that zone with the Harappans.

This does not mark the end of protohistoric horizons. On the contrary, there are columns of archaeological cultures with fairly continuous occupations that are visible well into the 1st millennium BCE. Those cultural horizons are not discussed here because the formidable data make even a summary presentation impossible. However, the sum total of the evidence that has emerged out of archaeological investigations strongly underlines that multiple lines of cultural development, rather than a unilineal pattern, are the dominant feature of the archaeology of protohistoric India.

Issue of Iron Technology

If this chapter began with an exposition of the paradigm shift that unfolded in understanding the advent of food production in India,

4.7 Excavations at Malhar. Photograph: Rakesh Tiwari.

4.8 Artefacts from Malhar. Photograph: Rakesh Tiwari.

4.9 Raja Nal-ka-Tila— excavations. Photograph: Rakesh Tiwari.

4.10 Raja Nal-ka-Tila—a view of the surroundings. Photograph: Rakesh Tiwari.

it ends with an elucidation of the definitive modifications that have emerged in assessing the advent of iron technology in India. Two of the assumptions that used to be made about its advent are worth mentioning. The first concerned its origins, where it was assumed that it was invented in West Asia, from where it moved to other parts of the world. In India, it was seen variously as having been brought by either the Aryans or the Achaemenids.[13] The second concerned the character of the changes that followed its introduction, where it was argued that iron technology was the key factor in the creation of a strong agricultural base in the Gangetic plains which, in turn, was crucial to the birth of cities circa 600 BCE.

From 1976 onwards, the archaeological evidence on a much earlier presence of iron in different parts of India began to be regularly pointed out which questioned both these assumptions.[14] By the early 1990s, the presence of occasional bits of iron in the context of Harappan sites like Lothal and Allahadino too was recognized. In fact, the first distinct phase in the development of a technology capable of producing metallic iron coincides with early chalcolithic cultures. Since then, important new evidence of an early use of iron in Uttar Pradesh, which covers large parts of the heartland of Gangetic India, has also emerged. There is iron in Black-and-Red Ware levels at Jakhera and at Dadupur, with three radiocarbon dates from the latter site hovering around 1700 BCE. Iron-bearing levels at Malhar (figures 4.7 and 4.8) and Raja Nal-ka-Tila (figures 4.9–4.11) are also fairly early. Malhar (II) which is iron-bearing, goes back to the early 2nd millennium BCE while Raja Nal-ka-Tila has been dated to circa 1300 BCE.[15] Both these sites show extensive evidence of iron smelting and manufacture. Finally, the antiquity of iron at Jhusi near Allahabad has also been put around the end of the 2nd millennium BCE. The plethora of dates has been mentioned to show that the use of iron in this part of the Ganga plains is likely to be as early as the 2nd millennium BCE. Places like Malhar and Raja Nal-ka-Tila probably supplied smelted bloomer iron to the central Ganga plains, which implies a distributive network that was already in place. This was many hundreds of years before the appearance of early historic cities there.

In the light of such data, the notion of the Iron Age representing a major social and economic transformation, as much as it may appeal to our love of a neatly ordered succession of events working in tandem with technological change, can no longer stand up to historical scrutiny.

Notes

1   C. Jarrige, J.F. Jarrige, R.H. Meadow and G. Quivron (eds.), *Mehrgarh Field Reports 1974–85: From Neolithic Times to the Indus Civilisation*, Karachi: The Department of Culture and Tourism, Government of Sindh, 1995.

2   For a summary, see R. Tewari, "The Beginning of Wheat, Barley and Rice Cultivation: Mehrgarh and Lahuradeva", in Dilip K. Chakrabarti and Makkhan Lal (eds.), *History of Ancient India Vol. II: Protohistoric Foundations*, New Delhi: Vivekananda International Foundation and Aryan Books International, 2014.

3   Dorian Fuller, Ravi Korisettar, P.C. Venkatasubbaiah and Martin Jones, "Early Plant Domestications in Southern India: Some Preliminary Archaeobotanical Results", *Vegetation History and Archaeobotany* 13(2–4), 2004, p. 126.

4   R.N. Kaw, "The Neolithic Culture of Kashmir", in D.P. Agrawal and Dilip K. Chakrabarti (eds.), *Essays in Indian Protohistory*, Delhi: B.R. Publishing Corporation, 1979, pp. 219–27.

5   See Dilip K. Chakrabarti, *India: An Archaeological History* (second edition), New Delhi: Oxford University Press, 2009, pp. 146–47, 216–21 and 331.

6   For the discovery of the Indus civilization, see Nayanjot Lahiri, *Finding Forgotten Cities: How the Indus Civilization Was Discovered*, New Delhi: Permanent Black, 2005.

7   For the main features of the Harappan civilization, see Dilip K. Chakrabarti (ed.), *Indus Civilization Sites in India: New Discoveries*, Mumbai: Marg, 2004; G.L. Possehl, *Indus Age: The Beginnings*, Philadelphia: University of Pennsylvania Press, 1999; J.M. Kenoyer, *Ancient Cities of the Indus Civilization*, Karachi: Oxford University Press, 1998. These are also books that contain all the references to the original reports and articles relating to a large number of Harappan sites.

8   B.B. Lal, Jagat Pati Joshi, A.K. Sharma, Madhu Bala and K.S. Ramachandran, *Excavations at Kalibangan: The Harappans (1960–69), Part I*, New Delhi: Archaeological Survey of India, 2015, p. 30. This report was finally published more than 45 years after the excavations.

9   Arunima Kashyap and Steve Weber, "Harappan Plant Use Revealed by Starch Grains from Farmana, India", *Antiquity* 84, 2010.

10 Randall William Law, *Inter-Regional Interactions and Urbanism in the Ancient Indus Valley: A Geologic Provenience Study of Harappa's Rock and Mineral Assemblage*, Kyoto: Indus Project, Research Institute for Humanity and Nature, 2011.

11 A good summary is available in Dilip K. Chakrabarti, *India: An Archaeological History*, chapter VI.

12 M.K. Dhavalikar, H.D. Sankalia and Z.D. Ansari, *Excavations at Inamgaon*, Pune: Deccan College, 1988.

13 N.R. Banerjee argued on behalf of the Aryans while D.H. Gordon and R.E.M. Wheeler suggested that iron was brought by the Achaemenids. For a summary, see Dilip K. Chakrabarti, *The Early Use of Iron in India*, New Delhi: Oxford University Press, 1992, pp. 16–18.

14 A definitive study of this issue, for instance, was published by Dilip K. Chakrabarti. See Chakrabarti, "The Beginning of Iron in India", *Antiquity* 50, 1976, pp. 114–24.

15 Rakesh Tewari, "Origins of Ironworking in India: New Evidence from the Central Ganga Plain and the Eastern Vindhyas", *Antiquity* 77, 2003, pp. 536–44; Rakesh Tewari, R.K. Srivastava, K.K. Singh and K.S. Saraswat, "Report on the Excavations at Raja Nal-Ka-Tila, District Sonbhadra, Uttar Pradesh (India): 1995–96–97", *Pragdhara* 21–22, 2010–12, pp. 1–226.

5 Historical India and Beyond

The advent of the early historic phase in large parts of India dates to the first half of the 1st millennium BCE, even while the dates and key features of this watershed process can be fairly varied depending upon the region. This chapter begins with an overview of what appear to be the significant elements in post-independence research on a variety of issues—from the beginning of writing to the nature of historic cities. Theoretically speaking, the historical archaeology of India includes and goes beyond that first phase of growth and consolidation. This means that it encompasses a range that stretches from ancient times to the archaeology of modern India. In reality, though, while there is an archaeological tradition of research on ancient historical India, what we know, through the lens of archaeology, about the historical periods that follow is sporadic. There is no professionalization visible here in relation to the various subdisciplines that constitute historical archaeology, such as industrial archaeology or medieval archaeology or the archaeologies of diaspora communities, which are subjects of specialized research elsewhere.

Early Historic India

The historical period begins with the advent of writing. A major landmark in understanding the archaeological evidence for its beginnings has come from Tamil Nadu. This concerns the Brahmi script, and firm evidence for dating its beginnings much prior to the Maurya epigraphs has emerged from excavations at two sites in Tamil Nadu—Porunthal and Kodumanal.

Porunthal is situated on the left bank of the Porunthilaru river in the foothills of the Western Ghats. The excavations of 2009–10 revealed a major glass-bead manufacturing centre with which were associated megalithic grave burials. Here, paddy grains collected from two graves have yielded two accelerator mass spectrometry (AMS) dates—490 BCE (calibrated 520 BCE) and 450 BCE (cal. 410 BCE).[1] The dates come from graves that contain potsherds bearing inscriptions in the Brahmi script. One of these yielded two kilograms of paddy grains which were placed in a four-legged jar, as also a polished red ware ring-stand engraved with a Tamil-Brahmi script inscription that reads "vi-y-ra" (figures 5.1–5.3).

Kodumanal is located on the north bank of the Noyyal river, a tributary of the Kaveri. Here too, the excavators have succeeded in obtaining early scientific dates. There are five AMS dates—of 200 BCE (cal. 200 BCE), 275 BCE (cal. 380 BCE), 300 BCE (cal. 370 BCE), 330 BCE (cal. 380 BCE) and 408 BCE (cal. 480 BCE)—from well-stratified layers at depths of 15, 60, 65, 80 and 120 centimetres respectively. These come from layers which have yielded a considerable number of potsherds bearing inscriptions in the Tamil-Brahmi script (figures 5.4 and 5.5). Around 100 such potsherds were found in 2012 alone, and on the whole the excavations have yielded 551 Tamil-Brahmi inscribed sherds. The excavations have also yielded five sherds of Northern Black Polished Ware (NBPW) which is associated with the first phase of the early historical period in north and central India. Considering that in earlier seasons silver punch-marked coins were found at Kodumanal, there is now excellent evidence to argue that this commercial centre had well-established trade and cultural contacts with the middle Gangetic plains in the 5th century BCE. Incidentally, there is still a 65-centimetre-thick cultural deposit that contained inscribed potsherds below the level which has yielded the above-mentioned dates, so there is every possibility that the beginning of the early historic period may be pushed back further.

Taken together, these sites have changed our understanding of the timing of the cultural transformation which constitutes the beginning of the early historical period in India. It used to be argued that south India entered into the

5.1 Porunthal—ring-stand inscribed in Tamil-Brahmi, reading "vi-y-ra". On the right, the top picture is a view of the excavated chamber where the inscribed ring-stand was found; the second shows the inscribed ring-stand before excavation; the third is a close-up of the inscription. Photograph: K. Rajan.

5.2 Porunthal—paddy collected from four-legged jar. Photograph: K. Rajan.

5.3 The four-legged jar and ring-stand found at Porunthal. Photograph: K. Rajan.

historical phase around the 3rd century BCE. This is because of the historical presence there of Emperor Ashoka of the Maurya dynasty, whose Brahmi inscriptions mention political entities in the deep south. Since those epigraphs were found in the adjacent regions of Karnataka and Andhra, it used to be argued that writing too was introduced into south India during his rule. The excavations at Porunthal and Kodumanal have rendered that understanding as entirely invalid.

In the case of other parts of India, though, the evidence is still limited. The circa 800 BCE presence of wood charcoal from bhurjapatra (birch paper, from the bark of the tree) that was recovered at Sringaverapura is important, but writing as a full-blown phenomenon in north India appears much later in the archaeological record.

The other element that comes to mind in relation to early historic India is the phenomenon of urban growth. We know of many more cities today, which helps to better understand the process of urban evolution in various regions. A few of these urban centres are worth mentioning: Sanghol and Ropar (Punjab); Purana Qila (Delhi); Semthan (Kashmir); Hastinapur, Ganwaria, Mathura, Kausambi, Ayodhya, Rajghat (figures 5.6. and 5.7), Sravasti and Sringaverapura (Uttar Pradesh); Rajgir, Patna, Balrajgarh and Vaishali (Bihar); Chandraketugarh and Tamluk (West Bengal); Sisupalgarh and Jaugarh (Odisha); Ujjain and Besnagar (Madhya Pradesh);

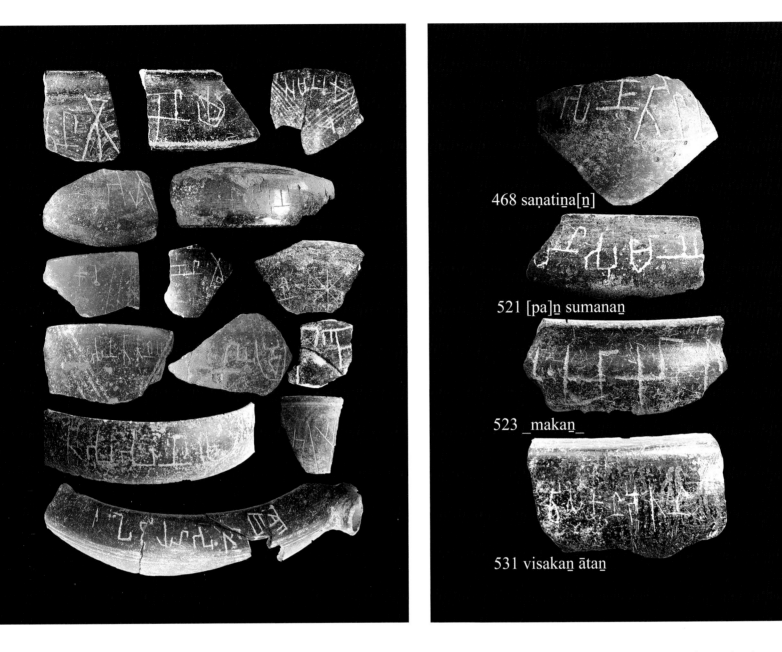

468 saṇatiṇa[ṇ]

521 [pa]ṇ sumanaṇ

523 _makaṇ_

531 visakaṇ ātaṇ

Bharuch (Gujarat); Pauni and Adamgarh (Maharashtra); Sannati and Chandravalli (Karnataka); Nagarjunakonda, Satanikota and Dharanikota (Andhra Pradesh); Kaveripattinam and Kodumanal (Tamil Nadu); and Pattanam (Kerala). Evidently, some states like Uttar Pradesh and Bihar are adequately represented, while in other regions like Kerala the picture is far more limited. In northeast India, a conscious search for early urban settlements has not yet begun. Considering the references to northeast India in different literary sources, the logical inference is that there should be a firm early archaeological basis for them, and exploring this dimension should be a priority area of research.[2]

There are a few general issues relating to historic cities that are worth highlighting.

Unlike pre-independence, the archaeology of historic cities has not been a priority area of research since 1947 and, consequently, there are hardly any city sites that have been horizontally excavated in the manner in which Harappan cities have since been uncovered. So, for instance, unlike the excavations of urban centres like Taxila or Bhita in the first half of the 20th century which resulted in structural remains that made their urban character palpable, most of the historic cities excavated since, because of the lack of horizontal digs, fail to conjure up the nature of their houses, streets, shops in an adequate way.

The nature of the Ikshavaku city of Vijayapuri that has been revealed at Nagarjunakonda is one of the few examples of a reasonably

5.4 Kodumanal—potsherds inscribed in Brahmi. Photograph: K. Rajan.

5.5 Kodumanal—potsherds inscribed in Tamil-Brahmi. Photograph: K. Rajan.

5.6 Rajghat—view of excavated remains. Photograph: Nayanjot Lahiri.

5.7 Rajghat—recently excavated remains including ring well. Photograph: Nayanjot Lahiri.

comprehensive documentation. The archaeology of political power as expressed in the ramparts and in the war memorials; the civic structures like the amphitheatre, roads, bathing ghats, tanks and a canal; the religious landscape made up of Hindu temples, Buddhist shrines and an ashvamedha (ritual sacrifice) site; and its economic vitality as expressed in the construction of a kind of dock where boats could be berthed, as also the shops and workshops—all of this forms part of a rich and variegated historical urban landscape.[3] The kind of detail revealed here is what is absent in our knowledge of most other urban centres excavated post-independence.

Usually, in relation to cities, it is important structural features at a few places that have generally been revealed. The tank complex at Sringaverapura is one of these which reveals excellent hydraulic engineering skills.[4] Water from the Ganga river in spate was taken through a special channel into a silting chamber, and then via an inlet channel into Tank A, and through a similar arrangement into Tank B. An interconnecting channel carried water to the circular Tank C in whose lower deposits, the presence of terracottas of Shiva, Parvati, Kubera etc. suggest a religious function. The full report of Sringaverapura, though, still awaits publication. In fact, what requires emphasis is the absence of definitive excavation reports for many of India's important urban centres. This is as true for Semthan in Kashmir as it is for Chandraketugarh in West Bengal. Finally, urban centres have to be visualized within the larger distribution of sites across the landscape. While in some parts, like segments of Uttar Pradesh, Haryana, Maharashtra and Tamil Nadu, studies of the site distribution pattern that go under the label of "settlement archaeology" have been done, in many other regions it is still not possible to conceive of the network of sites around the cities. Bairat, for instance, which is one of the only places where two Ashokan edicts were inscribed, was an important early historic place but there has been no detailed ground survey of its hinterland.

On the question of Ashokan inscriptions, our understanding of the archaeological landscape of the Maurya dynasty has been significantly extended because of many new epigraphic discoveries. The largest number of Ashokan edicts were discovered in Afghanistan between 1959 and 1973, and in Karnataka-Andhra between 1953 and 1989 (figures 5.8 and 5.9).[5] These have also been discovered in Madhya Pradesh, Uttar Pradesh and New Delhi. The most recent discovery of an Ashokan edict was made at Ratanpurwa in 2009, and considering how regularly Ashokan epigraphs keep popping out of places across South Asia, there is no reason to think of Ratanpurwa as the last in this very rocky path. These epigraphs, incidentally, have acquired a vivid resonance because the landscapes where they are imprinted, in many instances, have been explored. Our understanding of the Maski edict has been enhanced by what we know about a settlement, excavated in 1954, that existed in its vicinity. Similarly, archaeological investigations at Panguraria in central India, where a rock shelter was the locale for an edict, have revealed paintings in rock shelters and a Buddhist landscape of stupas and monastic cells. This is an important way through which inscriptional traces of the interventions of India's greatest ancient ruler have been historicized through archaeology.

5.8 Ashokan rock edict in the rock shelter at Panguraria. Photograph: Nayanjot Lahiri.

5.9 Stone bearing Sannati edicts of Ashoka, now at Kanaganahalli. Photograph: Nayanjot Lahiri.

What is noteworthy about the landscapes of historic India is that beyond cities and settlements, many sites of religion and ritual continue to be discovered. In the world of Buddhism, India's northeastern states are an example of this, an area that was earlier not known for Buddhist sites.[6] A pyramidal stupa was discovered and excavated in Meghalaya near the medieval township of Bhaitbari. In Tripura the remains of a 9th/10th century CE stupa were excavated at Shyam Sundar Tila in South Jolaibari (figures 5.10–5.12). Built in a cruciform plan, the outer walls of its basement bore decorated friezes of the Buddha, musicians, dancing

5.10 Shyam Sundar Tila with the cruciform plan evident. Photograph: S.B. Ota.

5.11 Decorated friezes on the basement wall of Shyam Sundar Tila. Photograph: S.B. Ota.

5.12 Detail of decorations on the basement wall of Shyam Sundar Tila. Photograph: S.B. Ota.

human figures, peacocks, a lion and a deer. Even in those regions where Buddhist remains have been unearthed since the 19th century, new stupa and monastic sites are still being discovered. At Satdhara, not far from Sanchi, in the middle of the 19th century, Alexander Cunningham had described the main stupa and the remains of some other buildings in its vicinity. In 1994, many new structures were discovered—as many as 40 stupas, as well as apsidal temples and monasteries.[7] Simultaneously two Buddhist paintings were discovered on the perpendicular cliff that overlooks the Halali river. The classical rendering of the Buddha and the letters of the Brahmi epigraph reveal that these are likely to be of Gupta antiquity. A stunning early centre of Buddhism has been revealed at Deur Kuthar, on a route which passed from Prayaga to Bagelkhand.[8] Of the four stupas, the most imposing is Stupa 1, surrounded by a Mauryan stone railing, with a height of more than 9 metres. Unlike other Mauryan sites marked by pillars, this Buddhist complex and its stone pillar had no connection with either a political group or a Mauryan emperor. The Brahmi inscription on the pillar is about its erection

and dedication by a Buddhist upasaka (a lay devotee of Buddha) and his disciples.

The archaeology of Hindu worship is also marked by a similar pattern: discoveries in known places and archaeological and structural traces of rituals in new landscapes. The numerous temples that have continued to be regularly unearthed in many parts of India remain a rich resource for understanding the archaeology of worship and character of artistic imagination—the post-Gupta Devrani-Jethani temples at Tala in Chhattisgarh, declared as protected monuments in 1983, exemplify this (figures 5.13–5.15).[9] The rendering of a range of fantastic human-animal-plant hybrid sculptures makes for a unique site which speaks volumes for ancient artistic imagination and the skills of sculptors.

The evidence of rituals conducted within temples that excavations have sometimes revealed is also worth highlighting, as in the case of the temple areas at Bhitari in north India.[10] The large terracotta bowls found there were probably used either to offer food to the deity or for the ritual feeding of large groups of worshippers or pilgrims. Similarly, at the

5.13 Tala—Jethani Temple remains. Photograph: Nayanjot Lahiri.

5.14 Devrani Temple, Tala—image of Bhutanatha (usually called Rudra-Shiva in descriptions of the temple). Photograph: Nayanjot Lahiri.

5.15 Naigamesha image from the Devrani Temple, Tala. Photograph: Nayanjot Lahiri.

well-known Parashurameshvara temple at Gudimallam in Andhra Pradesh, the remains of animals (domestic sheep and goats) sacrificed for the deity were found in the inner sanctum. Archaeological traces of public rituals outside temples have also been recovered. At Jagatgram in Uttarakhand, the excavated brick platforms which were in the form of the "syena" (hawk or eagle with spread wings), appear to have been connected with the ashva-medha sacrifice. Various kinds of oblations were usually offered at such sacrifices, though such evidence has not been recovered at Jagatgram. Sanghol in Punjab, however, has yielded large quantities of organic material from ritual fire altars (c. 100–300 CE), and a palaeobotanical

investigation revealed that this was of the type usually used in sacrifice (e.g. of various foodgrains such as rice, barley, black gram, lentils and sesame; edible fruits such as jujube, dates, almonds and fig; medicinal fruits and seeds like nutmeg, black pepper and basil; and charcoal). Such data make archaeologically alive, perhaps for the first time, the vivid descriptions in Hindu religious texts of elaborate sacrificial offerings and oblations.

Medieval India is still largely known through texts, epigraphs and architecture. What has post-independence archaeology added to our knowledge of it? For one, there are sites in different parts of India whose long occupational levels contain remains of the medieval

5.16 Champaner—medieval remains. Photograph: V.H. Sonawane.

5.17 Signet ring from Champaner. Photograph: V.H. Sonawane.

centuries—Hastinapur, Sonkh, Purana Qila, Bhagatrav, Pachrahi and Nagara are a few examples of sites that yielded such remains. For another, there are some medieval towns and cities where the method of study has been an exploration of topographic and archaeological features into which documentary references have been woven.[11] The horizontal excavation of Amir Manzil in Champaner revealed a representative elite/noble residential complex with its multiple rooms, a central pillared hall, mural paintings, water channels and pleasure gardens, hamam and stable (figure 5.16). Also, that the owner was Abdul Bak Safavi alias Baba Gulam Ali has been suggested by the presence of an inscribed silver signet ring found in the excavation of Amir Manzil (figure 5.17). Then, there are fortified sites with their defensive works, remains of structures and hydraulic architecture that have attracted some attention. Bekal fort in Kerala, for instance, excavated over four seasons (1997–2001), revealed residential and palace remains and a mint as also a temple complex that are dated to the 17th–19th centuries.[12] The identification of the mint, believed to have been established in the time of Tipu Sultan, was done on the basis of coins, ingots and ovens. The work done at Senji fort in Tamil Nadu is another example of an archaeological survey which, incidentally, was based on a comparison of the material vestiges with the information in texts.[13] The modifications made by engineers with the introduction of gunpowder into warfare have been mapped and the arrangements made for storing gunpowder have been carefully studied. Beyond defences, there are details relating to the design of rainwater

collection tanks and grain storage facilities, as also their holding capacities. Lal Kot in Delhi, a fort that is said to have been built in the 11th century and excavated between 1957–61 and 1991–95, has also revealed a large hydraulic structure ("Anangtal") in the form of a tank with walls, platforms and steps.[14] The fortifications there were originally of rubble stone over which, later, several courses of burnt bricks were added.

Beyond fortified sites, there are some other features that have come alive in specific regions. The archaeology of irrigation technology in Tamil Nadu, which includes an understanding of the various components involved in the construction of tanks from ancient times till the 19th century, along with the study of a large body of inscriptions on sluice pillars and stones near tanks, reveals the technological character and social features of water management there.[15] The study of stepwells in Gujarat—with their profuse structured steps, pavilions, pools and shrines—is also worth mentioning in the context of water structures.[16]

With regard to the settlement archaeology of medieval India, the most comprehensive work is the Vijayanagara Metropolitan Survey, a ten-year survey project which explored the metropolitan region (extending up to 600 sq. km) of the imperial capital of Vijayanagara.[17] More than 650 sites were recorded in the intensive survey area, with roughly 80 more documented in the extensive survey region. So, it is a very significant site density that emerged from the survey. They included defensive sites with bridges and gateways; sacred sites with temples, shrines and isolated images; craft

production sites; agricultural sites with canals, wells, reservoirs or tanks etc.; and settlements ranging from towns and villages to isolated houses and inhabited rock shelters. In certain instances, the places and settlements that occur in the thousands of inscriptions of the medieval period have been identified on the ground. One of these is of the Chalukyan empire's Sarasvata-mandala and its subdivisions in Gujarat where places mentioned in inscriptions were identified because of the similarity in names: for example, Dhanada is Dhanda and Varanavada is Varnavada.[18] In the case of Tamil Nadu, almost all the names found in the inscriptions have been identified.[19] The reason for such identification is because nearly 90 per cent of the villages have temples that contain inscriptions. Apparently, even the land boundaries mentioned in the inscriptions and copper plates have been identified. Considering the profusion of epigraphs, this kind of exercise needs to be done across India in a detailed and systematic way.

A great deal on the maritime links of different segments of medieval and modern India can be recovered by accelerating the work done through marine archaeology in India. Maritime and submerged sites and monuments, shipwrecks and their paraphernalia, from anchors to sunken cargo, form the subject matter of marine archaeology. While the significance of this subject is self-evident in India which has a coastline of more than 7500 kilometres, as a branch of study it began in a systematic way only in 1981 when S.R. Rao initiated it at the National Institute of Oceanography in Goa.[20] This was done with the financial help of the Indian National Science Academy, and regular funds were provided by the Department of Science and Technology. Since then, the Archaeological Survey of India has established a marine archaeology wing, centres have been created for marine archaeology in Tamil University and Andhra University, and the National Institute of Ocean Technology has been set up in Chennai. So, institutionally, there is a base for such research. The problem is in terms of the quantum of discovery and excavation, with the ASI, for instance, largely focusing on training programmes and not on large underwater explorations.

The major elements that have been unearthed through marine archaeological research appear to be largely medieval and early modern remains: a jetty and anchors of the early medieval and medieval period (9th–14th centuries) off Dwarka (figures 5.18 and 5.19); a historical period site near Khudar Dargah at Bet Dwarka that is submerged during high tide which yielded various remains like amphora sherds, anchors and lead ingots; triangular and "Indo-Arabian" type stone anchors at Somnath, similar to those at Dwarka and Bet Dwarka; a huge linear stone structure in the water, on the western side of Vijaydurg fort of Maratha times, which may have been constructed to damage enemy ships, along with anchors in the adjoining dockyard area; anchors of the early historic period at Sindhudurg fort; and a number of shipwrecks in Goa waters. Of these, the remains of the shipwreck off St George's Reef belong to the 19th century and contain material of the Basel Mission Company, while the Sunchi Reef wreck belongs to the early 17th century with remains that reveal Chinese ceramics, iron guns, glass bottles and Martaban pottery

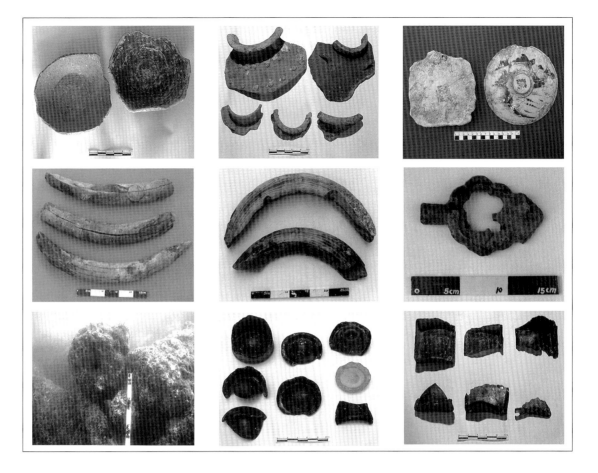

5.20 Sunchi wreck findings. Photograph: Sila Tripathi.

(figure 5.20). Shipwrecks have also been found in the Lakshadweep islands, with one which was a Greek ship carrying World War II surplus stores from Burma. Again, a brick structure has been found in the intertidal zone near Kaveripattinam (Poompuhar), while 3.5 kilometres from it a wooden hulled shipwreck of the late 18th century was found, the first wreck reported from the east coast of India.

Another new line of investigation which has yielded interesting results is the use of GIS and remote sensing for understanding the layout and character of historical sites and their landscapes. The analysis of such imagery around the massive monastic establishment of Nalanda, for instance, has yielded the shapes, location and layout of the tanks around it, and a 10-kilometre-long palaeochannel leading into the largest of these tanks (figure 5.21).[21] Again, in relation to one of the mounds, the digital elevation model suggested that there was the presence of a large four-pointed structure which was confirmed by a field investigation (figure 5.22). Remote sensing, particularly 3D visualization, has been used to understand the

impact of sea-level changes on coastal monuments around Mahabalipuram. Juxtaposing the present situation with an analysis of the Portolan chart of Mahabalipuram (dating from 1670) which shows the seven "Pagodas" highlights that the local coastline has changed over the intervening centuries.[22] The use of GIS along with other sources has also been used for studying the Lalbagh Botanical Garden in Bengaluru (figure 5.23).[23] The popular assumption is that the gardens laid out by Haidar Ali and Tipu Sultan in the 18th century are contained within the current boundary. However, an analysis of old maps, old paintings, satellite images and simulated views recorded in paintings using 3D virtual GIS concluded that Haidar and Tipu's gardens comprised five distinct plots, and only a portion of one of these garden plots overlaps with the modern Lalbagh.

Historical archaeology, though, remains to be pursued in a far more focused way. Aspects of the everyday lives of people, especially those who are rarely mentioned in written sources, the archaeology of warfare where artefacts and texts can be integrated, the study of early

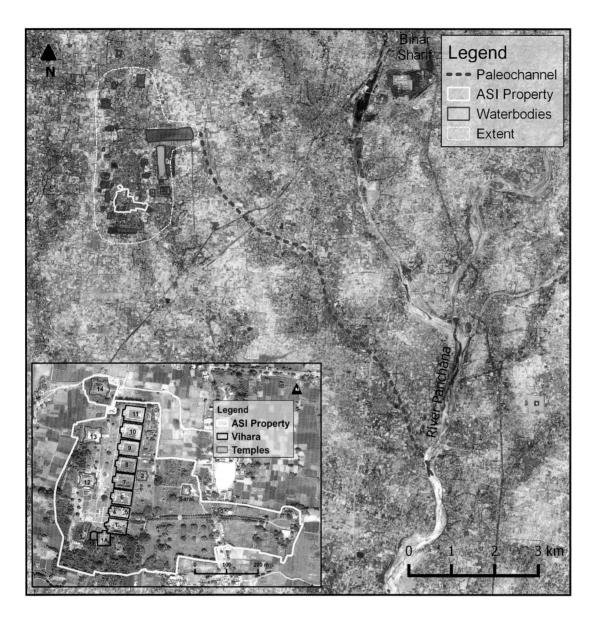

industrialization in India, the significance of extra-Indian contacts as reflected in the archaeological record of the medieval and early modern phases which goes beyond shipwrecks, the ways in which colonialism changed the countryside—all these are the subjects that can be meaningfully investigated. Research on these aspects, though, will only be seriously pursued when the importance of, and the study of, material remains beyond art and architecture are understood by scholars and students of medieval and modern India as being relevant for expanding the frontiers of research in their own fields.

Notes

1   K. Rajan, V.P. Yathees Kumar, S. Selvakumar, R. Ramesh and P. Balamurugan, "Archaeological Excavations at Porunthal, District Dindigul, Tamil Nadu", *Man and Environment* XXXVIII(2), 2013, pp. 62–85. The dates of Kodumanal in the following paragraph were emailed to me by K. Rajan.

2   Dilip K. Chakrabarti, *The Issues in East Indian Archaeology*, New Delhi: Munshiram Manoharlal, 1998, pp. 21–37.

3   K.V. Soundarajan (ed.), *Nagarajunakonda (1954–60)*, Vol. II, New Delhi: Archaeological Survey of India, 2006.

4   B.B. Lal, *Excavations at Sringaverapura (1977–86)*, Vol. I, New Delhi: ASI, 1993.

5   For a date-wise list, see the appendix in Nayanjot Lahiri, *Ashoka in Ancient India*, Ranikhet: Permanent Black, 2015.

6   For the references to sites mentioned in this paragraph, see Nayanjot Lahiri, "Before Buddhism, Beyond Buddhism: Aspects of the Archaeology

5.21 GIS map of Nalanda palaeochannel. Courtesy M.B. Rajani.

5.22 GIS map of Nalanda Begumpur mound. Courtesy M.B. Rajani.

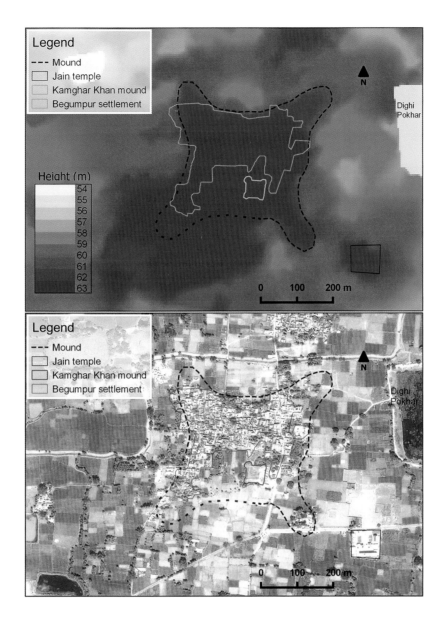

of Buddhism in India", *Pragdhara* 23, 2012–13, pp. 249–70.

7 R.C. Agrawal, "Stupas and Monasteries: A Recent Discovery from Satdhara, India", in Raymond Allchin and Bridget Allchin (eds.), *South Asian Archaeology 1995*, Vol. I, New Delhi: Oxford & IBH, 1997, pp. 403–15.

8 Phani Kanta Mishra, "Deorkuthar Stupa: New Light on Early Buddhism", *Marg* 52(1), 2001, pp. 64–74.

9 I owe the identification of what is called "Rudra-Shiva" as possibly an image of Bhutanatha to Professor Parul Pandya-Dhar, University of Delhi.

10 For the references to sites mentioned in relation to the archaeology of Hindu worship, see Nayanjot Lahiri and Elisabeth A. Bacus, "Exploring the Archaeology of Hinduism", *World Archaeology* 36(3), issue on *The Archaeology of Hinduism*,

edited by Elisabeth A. Bacus and Nayanjot Lahiri, 2004, pp. 313–25.

11 R.N. Mehta, "Ahmedabad: A Topographical, Toponymical and Archaeological Perspective", in B.M. Pande and B.D. Chattopadhyaya (eds.), *Archaeology and History: Essays in Memory of Shri A. Ghosh, Volume I*, Delhi: Agam Kala Prakashan, 1987, pp. 363–74. Among scholars, Mehta very early on focused on the importance of medieval archaeology; see, for instance, R.N. Mehta, *Medieval Archaeology*, New Delhi: Ajanta Publication, 1979. For Bhangarh, see C. Margabandhu, "An Archaeological Survey of Medieval Settlements (With Special Reference to Planning of Bhangarh Town, District Alwar)", *Puratattva* 44, 2014, pp. 29–42. For Champaner, see V.H. Sonawane, "Excavations at Champaner: A First World Heritage Site of Gujarat", *Puratattva* 39, 2009, pp. 68–79.

(a)

(b)

Lalbagh now
Lalbagh in 1799
Colebrook's view (179
Home's view (1792)

(c)

5.23 GIS map of Lalbagh,
Bengaluru. Courtesy M.B. Rajani.

12 M. Nambirajan, *Bekal Excavation (1997–2001)*, New Delhi: ASI, 2009.

13 Jean Deloche, *Senji (Gingee): A Fortified City in the Tamil Country*, Pondicherry: Ecole francaise d'Extreme-Orient Institut francais de Pondichery, 2005.

14 Buddha Rashmi Mani, *Delhi: Threshold of the Orient*, New Delhi: Aryan Books International, 1997.

15 K. Rajan, *Ancient Irrigation Technology: Sluice Technology in Tamil Nadu*, Thanjavur: Heritage India Trust, 2008.

16 Jutta Jain-Neubauer, *The Stepwells of Gujarat in Art-Historical Perspective*, New Delhi: Abhinav Publications, 1981.

17 Carla M. Sinopoli and Kathleen D. Morrison, *Vijayanagara Metropolitan Survey Volume I*, Ann Arbor MI: University of Michigan, 2007. Also see Carla M. Sinopoli, "Beyond Vijayanagara's City Walls: Regional Survey and the Inhabitants of the Vijayanagara Metropolitan Region", in Himanshu Prabha Ray and Carla M. Sinopoli (eds.), *Archaeology as History in Early South Asia*, New Delhi: Indian Council of Historical Research and Aryan Books International, 2004, pp. 257–79.

18 H.D. Sankalia, *Prehistoric and Historic Archaeology of Gujarat*, New Delhi: Munshiram Manoharlal Publishers Pvt. Ltd., 1987, chapter 26.

19 This was mentioned to me in an email with references by K. Rajan: "There is no specific book giving complete list of identification in the whole of Tamil Nadu but almost all the names found in the inscriptions are identified. The book like *Ancient Geography of Kongu Country* by K.S. Vaithyanathan gives complete list in Kongu country (Coimbatore, Erode, Tiruppur, Karur districts). Prof. Y. Subbarayalu *Political Geography of Chola Country (Thanjavur, Nagapattinam, Tiruvarur and part of Trichi districts)* gives complete list in Kaveri delta. Vedachalam thesis on Madurai region (Madurai, Virudhunagar districts), C. Santhalingam thesis on Tondaimadalam region (former North Arcot and South Arcot districts), R. Poongundran thesis on Tagadur region (Dharmapuri district), L. Thiyagarajan thesis on Ariyalur region (Ariyalur district) and likewise several Ph.D. thesis and M.Phil. thesis almost identified more than 90% of the villages mentioned in the inscriptions."

20 For details on marine archaeology in India, see Sila Tripathi, "An Overview of Maritime Archaeological Studies in India", in Sila Tripathi (ed.), *Maritime Contacts of the Past: Deciphering Connections Amongst Communities*, New Delhi: Kaveri Book Service, 2015, pp. 729–65; Sila Tripathi, "An Overview of Shipwreck Explorations in Indian Waters", in Sila Tripathi (ed.), *Shipwrecks around the World*, New Delhi: Prestige Books, 2015, pp. 783–810; Sila Tripathi, A.S. Gaur and Sundaresh, "Marine Archaeology in India", *Man and Environment* XXIX(1), 2004, pp. 28–41.

21 M.B. Rajani, "The Expanse of Archaeological Remains at Nalanda: A Study Using Remote Sensing and GIS", *Archives of Asian Art* 66(1), Spring 2016, pp. 1–23.

22 M.B. Rajani and K. Kasturirangan, "Sea-Level Changes and Its Impact on Coastal Archaeological Monuments: Seven Pagodas of Mahabalipuram", *Journal of the Indian Society of Remote Sensing*, Springer, Published online April 17, 2012, DOI 10.1007/s12524-012-0210-y.

23 Meera Iyer, Harini Nagendra and M.B. Rajani, "Using Satellite Imagery and Historical Maps to Investigate the Original Contours of Lalbagh Botanical Garden", *Current Science*, 102(3), February 10, 2012, pp. 507–09.

6

Protection of and Pressures on Monuments and Sites

The previous chapters have explored the material past of India, at least the key elements that have emerged out of post-independence research. What happens to such remains after their discovery and documentation is the focus here. How do sites get protected and conserved? What are the pressures on them and who bears responsibility for destruction when it takes place? These are issues that require introspection because the quantum expansion in archaeological research has not been followed up by adequate safeguards for the protection of what has been discovered—archaeological sites and features, monuments and relict architectural remains.

While there are safeguards in the form of legislation and in the network of agencies involved in heritage preservation, in terms of ground realities enforcement remains a major problem. The will to follow the rule of law, as this chapter reveals, is less than adequate across public life, including among the arms of the government.

Nor is the technical conservation work at a number of protected monuments of a quality that matches up to standards that are followed in many countries that have as rich and diverse a monumental legacy as India.

Protecting Monuments through Legislation

Archaeological sites and monuments have multiple guardians. The preeminent government department for protecting and conserving monuments is the Archaeological Survey of India, working under the Union Ministry of Culture. It protects 3650 monuments (according to its website) which have been brought under the ambit of the relevant legislation and declared as monuments of national importance. State and Union Territory Departments and Directorates of Archaeology, under their own legislations, protect monuments that are of state and regional importance, and if a combined list of these was generated, it would

6.1 The protected stupa site of Bakraur. Photograph: Nayanjot Lahiri.

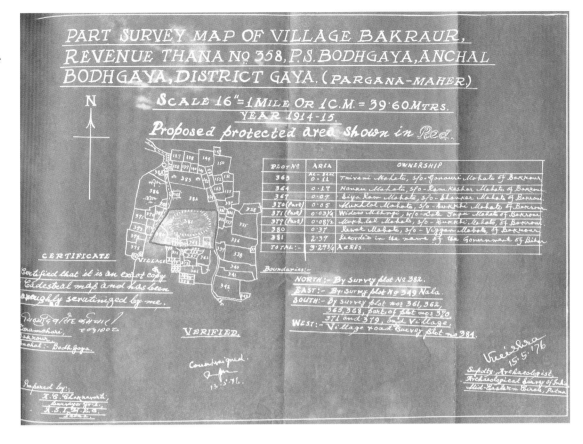

6.2 Survey map of Bakraur showing area to be brought under protection and the nature of its surroundings. Courtesy ASI.

cover more than 10,000 monuments. Under central and state lists, monuments include not merely structural remains, rock sculptures and caves but also monoliths, inscriptions, graves and mounds which have been in existence for not less than 100 years. Then, there are endowment act lists (mainly religious endowments) which include at least 12,000 historic structures. Not all monuments, though, find a place in such lists. The unprotected monuments that dot the Indian countryside would run into many lakhs. The records of the National Mission on Monuments and Antiquities noted some 500,000 unprotected monuments.

Protected monuments have three demarcated segments in and around them which are specified by legislation: a protected area, a prohibited zone and a regulated zone. The protected area is the monument itself, the prohibited zone is the area within a 100-metre radius around it where no new construction is allowed. The regulated zone of some 200 metres beyond the prohibited zone (which can be increased if necessary) requires clearance from the relevant authority before any change takes place within it. The purpose of this zoning is twofold. First,

it is supposed to protect sites that can be endangered by human activity. It is similar to the zoning around tiger reserves where a core area is set apart for the animals to live in, and where human disturbance is not permitted, while in the surrounding buffer zone, limited human activity is allowed. Second, it helps in providing an aesthetic perspective to monuments. Chapter 2 of this book has pointed out the genesis of this legislation in the Nehruvian years and chapter 8 will show how this was strengthened in 2010.

Who draws the attention of the state to these monuments and what are the steps by which these come to be protected? This has been done in a number of ways since 1947. Field researchers and excavators, in many instances, have set in motion the process for listing a site as protected. In 1976 the prehistoric potential of the megalithic site of Mottur in Tamil Nadu was brought to the attention of M.N. Deshpande, then Director General of the ASI, by B. Narasimhaiah, a technical assistant in the Survey.[1] More than a year later, the monuments were inspected and the area which was proposed for protection demarcated. Eight plots were sought to be protected of which six

6.3 Navaratna temple at Pathra. Photograph: Nayanjot Lahiri.

6.4 Another protected temple at Pathra. Photograph: Nayanjot Lahiri.

were held by private individuals who were to be offered compensation. These were to be acquired because the megaliths were being disturbed by ploughing, and dismantled for reuse in constructing rubble walls. Some five years later, the site was notified as protected.

The same process was followed at Bakraur in Bihar. In 1973–74, the ASI archaeologist K.M. Srivastava excavated the stupa site there—where he found epigraphic corroboration of its association with Sujata, the village woman who, according to the Buddhist tradition, had fed Siddhartha Gautama just prior to his enlightenment. While the excavations were in progress Srivastava wrote to Debala Mitra, then Director General of the ASI, asking that Bakraur be protected.[2] A blueprint was prepared which demarcated the boundaries for the purpose of protection (figures 6.1 and 6.2). Subsequently, a draft notification was issued and, eventually, Bakraur was declared protected on August 11, 1979.

Local pressure has also played an important role. In the case of the Gauri Sagar Tank at Sibsagar (Assam), it was the public of this locality, especially B.C. Neog, the Headmaster of the Gauri Sagar Industrial Institute, who took the initiative. In one of the representations that he sent to the Director General of the ASI on behalf of the people of the locality, his sense of pride in the tank and the urgency to repair it is palpable. As he put it, "the sea like tank at Gaurisagar is really a treasure to the nation", and its present condition was pathetic.[3] Similarly, the 30 or so terracotta temples at Pathra in West Bengal's Paschim Medinipur district were brought under the protective umbrella of the ASI because of an indefatigable local resident, Yeasin Pathan (figures 6.3 and 6.4). He began to make efforts from the 1970s onwards, appealing to state and central government authorities, as also setting up the Pathra Archaeological Preservation Committee. Eventually, his efforts resulted in some 20 lakhs of rupees being allotted for

temple restoration that was undertaken by the ASI. Incidentally, Pathan has also published, with support from the district administration, an archaeological list of several hundred sites in the district, extensively illustrated with photographs.[4]

Not every such attempt, though, results in places becoming monuments of national importance. There is, in fact, no shortage of characters who see antiquity in places where none exists, and ask for those to be declared as protected. There was an ex-army man, D.C. Chanan, who in 1977 wrote to the then newly appointed Foreign Minister Atal Behari Vajpayee about putting Daksha Mandir and Sati Kund in Hardwar on the Central list of protected monuments.[5] According to him, these places were "not only centuries old but belong to the Satyug Period even prior to Shree Ram Raj of Mahatma Gandhi Ji, and as such if neglected in the past, *should not* be totally ignored forever." An inspection by the ASI revealed that there

was hardly anything of archaeological importance, and the conclusion was that if at all there was to be some beautification, it ought to be undertaken by the state government. This left Chanan a miffed man, who then went on to protest strongly about how "two sacred places of Hindu Society are being ignored by the Hindu Government in Hindu India"![6]

Beyond institutions and individuals, many monuments have been protected because of political interest. This was precisely how the Hari Parbat fort in Kashmir came under the protection of the ASI. Situated on the southeastern outskirts of Srinagar, the hill has multiple associations, and is sacred to Hindus and Muslims (figure 6.5). There is a temple dedicated to the goddess Sharika on the western slope while on the southern slope is the shrine of the Muslim saint Hazrat Maqdoom Sahib (figure 6.6). Dara Shukoh, eldest son of Emperor Shah Jahan, also built a mosque at its base in honour of a Sufi saint who was a spiritual guide to him. The fort

6.5 View from the top of the Hari Parbat fort. Photograph: Abdul Rashid Lone.

6.6 Shrine of Hazrat Maqdoom Sahib below the fort at Hari Parbat. Photograph: Abdul Rashid Lone.

itself goes back to Mughal times, with some additions made to it in the 18th century during Afghan rule. In the 19th century, it passed to the Dogras—when a temple was added to it, as also long barracks. There is also a two-room structure just on the left side of the main gate which apparently was the prison cell of the Kashmir leader Sheikh Mohammad Abdullah during his "Quit Kashmir" campaign (figure 6.7).

Whether it was his personal association or the neglected state of the fort, or both, in 1977 Sheikh Abdullah who by then had become the Chief Minister of Jammu and Kashmir sought central protection for Hari Parbat fort (figure 6.8).[7] Some months before this, he had toured some of the archaeological sites in and around Srinagar with the Director General of the ASI, and had been very impressed with the fort's archaeological and historical character. Soon enough, this came under central protection.

The Role of Non-Governmental Organizations

Beyond those monuments which are given protection under the central act, non-governmental organizations (NGOs) have intervened in significant ways to protect the built heritage of a number of cities and towns. The most well known and largest NGO, one that has a pan-India reach, with chapters in 170 Indian cities, is the Indian National Trust for Art and Cultural Heritage (INTACH). Set up in 1984 with the mission to conserve heritage, tangible and intangible, it has helped in heritage property conservation and restoration in many states and union territories.

Much before the founding of INTACH, a movement for the protection of built heritage began in Bombay. More than any other city, it was Bombay that had seen a large number of heritage structures being pulled down, and as a consequence the Save Bombay Committee was created there in 1973. This was followed by the founding of the Bombay Environmental Action Group (BEAG) in 1979. Thanks to the BEAG's efforts, the Heritage Regulations for Greater Bombay were passed by the Maharashtra state government in 1995. The pulls and pressures, the negotiations and meetings, the setbacks before and after these regulations were passed, are very well captured in the 2007 book *Heritage and Environment: An Indian Diary* by Shyam Chainani, who was himself a pioneer and participant in this heritage movement.

6.8 Chief Minister Abdullah's letter to Union Minister of Education, Nurul Hasan about Hari Parbat. Reproduced from ASI file.

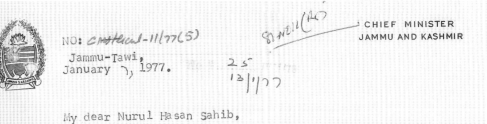

CHIEF MINISTER
JAMMU AND KASHMIR

NO: CM/Local-11/77(5)

Jammu-Tawi,
January 7, 1977.

My dear Nurul Hasan Sahib,

In early November last year, I had an occasion to visit some of the archaeological sites in Srinagar when Mr. Deshpandey Director General, Archaeological Survey of India, who happened to be there, also accompanied me. Among other sites visited was the Hari Parbat Fort. This is the only surviving medieval Fort commanding panoramic view of the Valley. It is built atop the hillock known as Hari Parbat by non-muslims and Kohi-maran by the Muslims of Kashmir. A detailed note giving the background information of this Fort prepared by Mr. C.L. Suri, Superintending Archaeologist, Archaeological Survey of India, J&K Region, is enclosed. Considering the historical importance and its potential as a place of tourist attraction, I suggested to Mr. Deshpandey that the Fort might be declared as a national protected monument including the wall around it. The Fort is at a very convenient distance from the city of Srinagar and can be reached by motor transport very easily. My idea was that it could be developed as a place of tourist attraction if it is flood lit during nights and other beautification works, as indicated to Mr. Deshpandey on spot, when he visited the site with me, could be carried out. Mr. Deshpandey also agreed that it was a very good idea to throw it open to tourists, and in that context, it was very necessary to restore its pristine character. It is true that Archaeological Survey of India have undertaken repairs of the wall near the main gate but it involves repairs and restoration work on a massive scale. I also enclose photographs of the Fort which will give some broad idea of the archaeological and historical character of this Fort. I shall indeed appreciate if you kindly have it declared as a national protected monument along with the wall around it.

With kind regards,

Yours sincerely,

(S.M. Abdullah)

Prof. S. Nurul Hasan,
Union Minister for Education,
New Delhi.

As the book highlights, what worked most satisfactorily was when an NGO and a government department came together with a common purpose. The protection of the forts on the islands of Underi and Khanderi, one owing its origin to the Siddis and the other a Konkani fortress, is an instance of this. Apparently, in 1978, there was a plan by the Rashtriya Chemicals & Fertilizers to construct a jetty, which would run from Thal to Underi—endangering it—and from there to the sea. It was the initiative, at the behest of the BEAG, of A.P. Jamkhedkar, Director of Maharashtra

Government's Department of Archaeology and Museums, that resulted in the forts getting declared as protected monuments. Of course, as Chainani pointed out, while these came to be protected, there are thousands of other forts and remains in Maharashtra which lie completely unprotected.

Vishrambag Wada in Pune was also saved in a similar way. Built in the early part of the 19th century by the last Peshwa for his vishram (relaxation), the Wada later housed a number of government offices. In 1979, it was decided that it would be demolished and replaced by a multistoreyed building. Because of Chainani's intervention, Sadashiv Gorakshkar, Director of the Prince of Wales Museum (now CSMVS, Mumbai), took up the matter in the State Archaeology Advisory Committee, which strongly recommended that protection be accorded to the Wada. Many years later, Jamkhedkar recalled his own role in the process:

> On receiving complaints, both from individuals, and from newspaper reports, in January 1979, I sent a team to inspect the monument and decided to prepare a plan for its protection. During my visit to Poona in August, I telephoned the Collector and apprised him of the state of the monuments. On a request from the Department of Archaeology, the Collector wrote to the Muncipal Commissioner to stop the demolition…. The preliminary notification for protection was issued in 1980. The Municipal Corporation objected saying that there were government offices inside

the monument and asked for protection to be given to part of the monument. However, the full monument was declared a protected monument.[8]

In Champaner as well, the Heritage Trust of Baroda has worked steadily for the protection of the site. Its efforts were crucial in getting the Champaner-Pavagadh area declared a World Heritage Site by UNESCO in 2006. A requirement for that designation was a comprehensive management plan. This was drafted by the Trust and passed in November 2006 as "The Champaner-Pavagadh Archaeological Park World Heritage Area Management Authority Act 2006". Incidentally, this act has overriding powers over other Gujarat acts.

Heritage lists have been prepared by NGOs in many instances for different historic cities and towns ranging from Pune to Hyderabad. However, in the absence of legal protection, the lists by themselves, are not enough to ensure protection.

6.9 Gaya Museum facade. Photograph: Nayanjot Lahiri.

6.10 and 6.11 Gaya Museum occupied by security personnel during Pitra Paksha ceremonies in 2012. Photographs: Nayanjot Lahiri.

Pressures on Monuments

The mere fact that a monument has been declared as protected or put on a notified list does not ensure that it will be properly conserved. In fact, the track record of government agencies in maintaining protected places of historic interest, to put it most charitably, is an indifferent one. This can be observed in all parts of India, and here one is not even drawing detailed attention to the ways in which the executive arm of government uses museums and monuments for purposes that have very little to do with their character and ambience. The photographs that capture the occupation of Gaya Museum by security personnel, on the instructions of the district authorities, during the Pitra Paksha ceremonies in Gaya in October 2012 are enough to underline such misuse (figures 6.9–6.11).

The lack of adequate conservation and cleanliness at monuments has been pointed out on many occasions by citizens, both powerful and ordinary. Among these, the letter of Major General K.S. Randhawa to the ASI poignantly sums up what such neglect implies. Randhawa had gone to Lucknow in December 1985, and used the opportunity to visit the Residency there (figure 6.12). It turned out to be an appalling experience. His letter is worth quoting in some detail:

> I am writing of my own accord as an individual citizen to say that as someone dedicated to history, it pained me to see how ill kempt the whole place is and what havoc has been played since I last saw it in 1952. It were as if we are reconciled to wish away this bit of our history, simply because of the British connection. I do not think that one can wish away or ignore any period, however traumatic it may be. Each reflects periods of glory and periods of subservience. How will our children's children be told of the siege and surge of nationalist feelings and equally how will they ever know what the British were and who was who among them.
>
> … It is a cruel joke to charge 50 paise even if so little, for a glimpse of this sad state of affairs. May I as an Indian citizen request you and the ASI Delhi to kindly give this thought so that our history is not lost to us. So that we will not have to go to London to know of Lucknow history and future generations will not forgive us.[9]

It is not merely relics of British India, about which Randhawa spoke so feelingly, that have suffered this fate. This is also true for many famous ancient monuments. During her tours across India, Indira Gandhi as Prime Minister made it a point to visit monuments, and followed up with letters to various authorities providing eye-witness accounts of the state of affairs there. For instance, her visit to Elephanta

6.12 Lucknow Residency today.
Photograph: Nayanjot Lahiri.

in 1974 resulted in a letter to V.P. Naik, Chief Minister of Maharashtra, where she pointed out the squalor of the surroundings in no uncertain terms. As she put it,

> The Trip to Elephanta was very pleasant but I was shocked to see how dirty the surroundings are. Empty coconut shells, paper, tins and all kinds of things were strewn around. The toilets were also very dirty with broken seats and the flush not working. When I spoke about this to the person who was with us, he thought he should have cleaned up for my visit. It is not at all important how things look when I go. What is important is the impression our visitors—especially foreign—take with them. I am strongly of the view that if it is not possible to keep such places clean, it is better to close them down to tourist traffic.[10]

Usually, monuments are spruced up when there are visiting dignitaries but, in this instance, the eagle-eyed Prime Minister cared to look beyond the cave itself and picked out all the dirt in the public areas and toilets.

In many instances, the squalor at protected sites is because of the absence of watch and ward staff. This has been the situation for decades. In 1987, in reply to a question by S.S. Ahluwalia in the Rajya Sabha, the government of the day accepted that of the 3521 protected monuments and sites, 1181 were without monument attendants.[11] Since then, the situation has only worsened. In 2010, the ASI stated on record that its staff strength did not permit the deployment of even a single person on a regular/full-time basis at more than 2500 of its monuments. This means that more than two-thirds of India's centrally protected monuments are poorly guarded.[12] This state of affairs is witnessed at several state-protected monuments. My personal experience during fieldwork in the Junagadh district of Gujarat in 2011 confirmed this. On paper, there was an impressive list of monuments that are supposedly protected by the state department of archaeology—without a single employee to man them. Beautiful monuments like the Pancheshwar caves, as a consequence, had been turned into rubbish dumps (figure 6.13).

Beyond institutional neglect, pressures on monuments have come from religious communities. This is true for protected sites with Hindu and Jain religious structures in many parts of India—from temples in Bhubaneswar in Odisha to caves at Udayagiri in Madhya

6.13 Pancheshwar caves in Junagadh district, a state-protected monument (mis)used as a rubbish dump. Photograph: Nayanjot Lahiri.

Pradesh, and beyond. This is also true for nationally protected mosques. A large number of mosques under the protection of the ASI are places which are not worship areas in the strict sense since no prayers have been offered there for a long time. However, such mosques have been under pressure for many decades now. In September 1983, for instance, the All India Muslim Majlis-e-Mushawarat (based in Delhi) submitted a memorandum to Prime Minister Indira Gandhi with three specific demands: "(1) that the Government should restore to the Muslim Community their constitutional and religious right of offering Namaz in the protected mosques, (2) that the Government should allocate due resources for maintenance and repair of protected mosques, and (3) that the attendants employed to look after their maintenance should be Muslims." When the Prime Minister did not yield, it was decided to increase the level of agitation by resolving, among other things, that the leaders of the Mushawarat, heads of Muslim organizations and Muslim Members of Parliament would perform their Friday prayers on March 2, 1984 in the Safdarjung mosque in violation of the existing ban, and court arrest. Indira Gandhi's letter of February 26 to the Mushawarat Convenor offered to hold further

discussions on this matter, even as it pointed out the logic of its position:

As you know, the Government is deeply interested in the rights of the minorities and does not interfere in their or anyone's worship. However, we are also concerned about our ancient monuments. Some mosques have not so far been used to offer prayers. They are your heritage and also the entire country's. I am told that holding prayers will require certain amenities, additions and structures which gradually change the original character of these mosques and destroy their historical importance and value. I cannot believe that is what your community would want to do.[13]

The discussion that took place between the delegation of the Mushawarat and ministers in Mrs Gandhi's government eventually resulted in prayers being offered at Safdarjung mosque on March 2, but the versions of what was agreed upon were diametrically different. The government refused to prepare the minutes of the meeting and merely noted that they had orally agreed to prayers being offered as a one-time symbolic gesture only. The Mushawarat, on the other hand, in their press release, maintained that apart from this there was an agreement in principle on the performance of namaz in any protected mosque, although care had to be taken that there would be no structural changes. There are many twists and turns in this story, but what is worth mentioning is that the general problem of pressure on protected monuments (that in this case happened to be mosques) was later flagged as a major issue of contention by Prime Minister Manmohan Singh. That the government was able to withstand the enormous pressure to open up monuments for religious use was seen by him as a significant achievement of his tenure as Prime Minister when he also happened to hold charge as Minister of Culture.[14]

A major problem with regard to several protected sites is that of encroachments. These take various forms, ranging from constructions on the site area to those in the prohibited and regulated zones. Hastinapur is an example of this where a number of encroachments have come up with complete impunity on the mounds that make up the site, ranging from a temple to the statue of a former legislator. In many instances, this happens because of the value of the land on which the monuments are constructed. In the case of the Tughluqabad fort in Delhi, 928 of the 2661 bighas of land transferred to the ASI after demarcation in 2000 were under encroachment. The encroachments were part of a systematic land grab by the land mafia with the help of what were described as "local residents" and "influential people", with the intention being to then sell the property.[15]

The problem of encroachment is compounded by the lack of support for the ASI from the executive authority. This is evident from the details of action initiated by the ASI, for instance, in its Delhi Circle where between 2003 and 2006, as many as 1171 First Information Reports (FIRs) were filed against individuals and entities who had built unauthorized constructions in the prohibited/regulated areas of centrally protected monuments.[16] These, in many cases, were followed by show cause notices and intimation to the concerned civic agencies. However, the support required from such agencies to execute demolition orders was largely missing.

Other instances reveal that sometimes politicians support the interests of encroachers at protected sites. India's top political leadership from Nehru to Manmohan Singh has generally been sensitive to the importance of preserving archaeological and architectural remnants of the past. This, though, cannot be said for all rungs of the political leadership and, in fact, there are instances where state leadership has attempted to push the central government to allow the destruction of protected sites. The appeal made by the Chief Minister of Haryana, Bhupinder Singh Hooda, is a most recent example of this where he sought the intervention of the Union Minister of Culture to get Khokra Kot denotified. The mound was under central protection but over the decades, more than 4000 residential and commercial buildings had come up within the prohibited area. Hooda's intervention was a result of notices of demolition that the residents had received, following court orders. Curiously, the Chief Minister not only pointed to the possibility of this giving rise to communal tensions and the fact that "poorer sections' demolition of houses would go against the policy of the Government itself", he also argued that nothing of national importance remained there since the artefacts had been taken away by professionals.

In order to ascertain the ground realities, a team from the ASI visited the site in July 2009. Their report highlighted the range of the cultural evidence there. Khokra Kot, as they pointed out, had an antiquity that went back to Harappan times, with a sequence that continued from the time when it was the capital of the Yaudheya Janapada till the 10th century CE. It also highlighted the chronology of encroachment. Till the 1970s, the site was relatively free of encumbrances, with only some 60 squatters. In 1988, the number had gone up to 438 and by 2004, 1654 houses had been built upon the site.[17] This had happened through illegal sale and purchase. The vivid details provided in the report show the organized land mafia at work and the connivance of local authorities:

It appears that the encroachment on large scale have taken place during the last 10 years by the land mafia and colonizers. Local authorities/administration/police, etc. have not acted upon at all even to check and restrict the menace, as the plot-owners are having Power of Attorney executed through property dealers. The names of newly developed colonies are Bhaum Nagar, Rohtas Nagar, Fatehpuri, etc. Majority of the houses are built on 100 sq. mt. size plots which vary in area from 75 to 300 sq. mts. Besides there are shops, schools, medical stores, dispensaries and a few religious structures. There are about 1742 encroachments as per the survey conducted in 2007 which might have now increased to more than 2000 as many of the existing buildings seem to be newly constructed.… Majority of the structures are of brick masonry with RCC roof. Some of the encroachers have raised a boundary wall with single room on their plot. The houses have regular water and electric/telephone connections. A few of the roads are metalled.[18]

This report was sent to the Chief Minister by Prime Minister Manmohan Singh (who was then also Minister of Culture). Singh noted that in the light of the facts mentioned in it, he hoped that Hooda would "appreciate that it would not be proper to denotify this site of great historical importance and which finds mention even in the *Mahabharata*".[19]

If the value of the land is one reason for encroachment and destruction, the other is profit to be gained from artefacts that emerge out of protected sites. This has, on many occasions, resulted in rampant destruction by gangs of the smuggling mafia. The instances of such destruction in the Mathura district are particularly notorious. This account of looting at the protected site at Ganeshra highlights the criminal modus operandi:

…the Gram Pradhan, Shri Kishan Lal, Chowkidar Shri Teja and other villagers of the Ganesra village told me that a gang

consisting of 20 unidentified persons entered the village in two cars, one motor cycle, one scooter, one tractor with trolly [sic], along with a bulldozer at about 8 p.m. on 23.1.83. They were carrying with them fire arms i.e. rifles, 12 bore guns, pistols etc. They fired few shots in the air and shouted that "nobody should come out or approach us" and also challenged the villagers if they have any courage, to "come out and obstruct us." The miscreants went to the Dhumari mound and lit petromaxes and put to fire several pits of dried cowdung cakes one by one which were stacked by the villagers on this mound. They started to ravage the mound by running the bulldozer in order to rob valuable sculptures and antiquities. As told by the villagers the whole operation took about 5 to 6 hours and then the miscreants left the village.[20]

There was no monument attendant posted at Ganeshra and it had only rarely been inspected by the conservation assistant. Moreover, even while it was protected, it had not been surveyed, nor was there a site plan.

What happened at Ganeshra in 1983 was soon repeated at protected mounds at Girdharpur and Chaubara in the Mathura district. In February 1986, more than half of the remains were cut up and truckloads of antiquities carted away for sale. Clearly, it is criminal gangs who in such instances have carried out large-scale destruction, and they are almost never apprehended.

Finally, there are protected sites where the character of monuments has changed through atrocious conservation work. Having seen a fair number of monuments across the country, it is possible to say with some confidence that there is no protocol followed across India for conservation and restoration. If the old fabric in many instances is maintained, in other cases, restoration work results in the disappearance of old features (see figures 7.3 and 7.4 for the example of the Tripolia gateway in Delhi).

A particularly appalling example of conservation comes from the Sannati area of

Karnataka, excavated in the 1990s. Sannati stands out because of the cluster of stupas (one of which, Kanaganahalli, has exquisitely carved panels reminiscent of Amaravati), mounds, fortifications, Ashokan edicts and more than 75 other inscriptions, scattered across an area of 10 square kilometres. Notwithstanding its outstanding remains exposed some 20 years ago, systematic conservation work has not yet begun there. I say this on the basis of my field observations, and this is what the report of the Department of Revenue, Government of Karnataka had to say about the state of the site:

> …hundreds of statues, panels, pillars, pedestals, capitals, cornices and inscriptions on the easily erasable limestone are still lying on the open ground exposed to the unbearable Gulbarga Summer and Winter and the vagaries of river Bhima which flows close by…. The ASI is far away in Delhi and its local officers are too powerless to influence their headquarters to fund this gigantic task. The State Department of Archaeology, as it functions today, is incapable of doing anything there or anywhere. Are we Kannadigas so careless and insensitive to the precious heritages of our past getting wasted that way? *How does one explain this abysmal neglect?*[21]

Kanaganahalli, in fact, typifies everything that is wrong about Indian archaeology and conservation post-independence. The excavation report was published some 15 years after it was dug out. Some of the sculptural repair that I saw on panels in 2010 looked like vandalism masquerading as conservation. The Ashoka panel, for instance, where the head of Ashoka's queen had been defaced by a resin lump, is reminiscent of how potholes on roads are repaired rather than how precious sculpture ought to be mended (figure 6.14). Worse was to come. Because of the celebrations around the ASI's 150th anniversary, a few of the Kanaganahalli panels were selected for replicas to be made. The "mother" moulds, from what senior officers of the government observed during their visits, were fabricated

out of fibreglass. This is a tricky material to work with and, for that reason, sculptors do not usually use it for making mother moulds even of modern sculpture. What is certain is that this was used here, and in the process of removing the moulds, the panels got chipped because bits remained stuck to them.

While the present state of conservation at Kanaganahalli remains unknown to me, I can only hope that this exquisite Buddhist site does not become independent India's Amaravati—a place which is remembered as much for its

6.14 Repair of the head of Ashoka's queen on the Kanaganahalli panel. Photograph: Nayanjot Lahiri.

exceptional heritage as for its wanton destruction by the very people who were meant to be its guardians. In the case of Amaravati, it was British archaeologists and officials who were responsible. Kanaganahalli, on the other hand, is a case where independent India's monument guardians have presided over a similar destruction.

Notes

1. For correspondence relating to Mottur, see ASI File No. 2/12/76-M, Volume II (B), Protection of Megalithic Burials, where a monolithic anthropomorphic figure is enclosed at Mottur Vellur—Vellur village.

2. Details relating to Bakraur are from ASI File No. 2/36/73-M. Protection and Conservation of the Ancient Site of Bakraur (Bodh Gaya).

3. ASI File No. 2/35/76-M. Protection of Gauri Sagar Tank, Sibsagar, Assam. Petition from Shri B.C. Neog, headmaster Gauri Sagar Industrial Institute to Director General, ASI.

4. Yeasin Pathan, *Archaeological List Map of District Paschim Medinipur West Bengal*, Paschim Medinipur: Paschim Medinipur Saksharata O Roge Pratished Samity Midnapore, 2007. This report also contains a narrative description of Pathra and its history of conservation. The saga of Pathan's endeavour to protect the Pathra temples has been widely reported in the popular media as well.

5. ASI File No. 2/21/77. Letter from D.C. Chanan dated March 29, 1977 to A.B. Vajpayee, Foreign Minister, Government of India.

6. ASI File No. 2/21/77. Letter from D.C. Chanan to the Director (Monuments), ASI, along with copies to Chief Secretary, Education Minister and Foreign Minister.

7. ASI File No. 11/77 (5). Letter from S.M. Abdullah, Chief Minister, Jammu and Kashmir dated January 7, 1977 to Nurul Hasan, Union Minister of Education, New Delhi.

8. Quoted in Shyam Chainani's *Heritage and Envi-*

ronment: An Indian Diary, Mumbai: Urban Design Research Institute, 2007, p. 413.

9. ASI File No. F.14-102/85. Complaint regarding bad maintenance of Lucknow Residency, its museum and the cemetery close by.

10. ASI File No. 25/3/75 M (T). The letter is dated December 20, 1974.

11. ASI File No. 34/16/87-M. Reply to Rajya Sabha Starred Question No. 3433 regarding watchmen of ancient monuments for March 11, 1987.

12. This was stated before the government-appointed Moily Committee in February 2010.

13. ASI File No. 20/2/91-M.

14. Author's conversation with Dr Manmohan Singh in September 2014.

15. All these details are from a reply to Rajya Sabha Unstarred Question Dy No. 2210 for November 27, 2000 asked by Ram Gopal Yadav, MP.

16. These details were provided by the ASI in 2010 to the government-appointed committee headed by M. Veerappa Moily, to analyse the impact of amendment to the AMASR Act 1958, including the impact of the AMASR (Amendment & Validation) Ordinance 2010.

17. All details pertaining to Khokra Kot, including quotations, are from ASI File No. 43-42/2008-M. De-notification of ancient site Khokra Kot for providing relief to people of that area from the fear of demolition of their houses.

18. This is from the status report in ASI File No. 43-42/2008-M.

19. Letter in the above-mentioned file by Prime Minister Manmohan Singh dated October 16, 2009.

20. This is from the inspection note of P.B.S. Sengar, Deputy Superintending Archaeologist Northern Circle (Agra) dated February 7, 1983 in ASI File No. 15/4/83-M.

21. "A Project for The Restoration, Preservation & Development of Buddhist Monuments in and around Sannati", Department of Revenue, Government of Karnataka, no date. Emphasis in original.

7 Auditing Archaeology and Museums

What has been described in the previous chapter on the challenges that face India's monuments, highlights instances that have been gleaned from letters and notings buried in the files of the Archaeological Survey of India. While these are significant in terms of what they reveal, the files themselves are accessible only to those individuals who have permission to examine them. Within the ASI and state archaeological agencies, there is no mechanism for regularly and publicly scrutinizing the state of the nation's archaeological heritage. This situation is qualitatively different as far as the state of India's economy or its environment is concerned, where reports are regularly compiled, made available in the public domain, and vigorously debated. Till that is done, the only kind of auditing of archaeology and museums—where findings are put in the public domain—is that which emanates from special committees set up by the government and by constitutional bodies like the Indian Parliament and the Comptroller and Auditor General of India.

The objective of this chapter is to look at what these auditors tell us about the state of Indian archaeology, monuments and museums. Their scrutiny of India's heritage, as will be evident, has generally been excellent, even while their recommendations have often remained unimplemented.

Committee Scrutiny

For more than 50 years, government-appointed and parliamentary committees have examined the functioning of the ASI. The first such assessment by an "Archaeological Review Committee" was done in 1965. Set up by the Government of India, the committee was chaired by Mortimer Wheeler, a former Director General of the ASI, with three university professors as members, and their report was submitted in the same year. An independent exercise was carried out some years later, in 1973–74, by parliamentarians who

were members of the Estimates Committee of the Fifth Lok Sabha. Under the chairmanship of R.K. Sinha, this committee produced a comprehensive 165-page report. This was followed ten years later by the report of the Expert Group on Archaeology appointed by the Government of India under the chairmanship of Ram Niwas Mirdha. For some unexplained reason, there was a gap of more than 20 years between this report and the next one tabled in November 2005 by the Parliamentary Standing Committee on Transport, Tourism and Culture, headed by Nilotpal Basu. There are critical observations, exhortations and recommendations in these reports. The problem, however, has been the lack of political will in implementing many of the recommendations.

Take the case of the Wheeler-headed committee. That the committee was certainly anxious to soothe the feathers of the ASI is evident, among other things, from its statement that it had "complete faith in the integrity, liveliness and devotion of the Survey's staff". Even so, it highlighted a range of problems and challenges facing the ASI. This included its lack of confidence in the ASI's capability of carrying out its national responsibility of conserving India's heritage, the grave arrears in the publication of its reports, the need for an Archaeological Science Laboratory, the lack of trained personnel in the states, the urgent need for an architectural survey of selected Indian domestic buildings "rapidly disappearing without record", and the necessity of encouraging the archaeology of medieval and later periods.[1]

Nearly ten years after it was submitted, an "action taken" report by the Ministry of Education and Social Welfare revealed that of the 21 recommendations made by the committee, action had only been taken on nine, while action on five of them was then under consideration.[2] The remaining seven recommendations were proposed to be taken up during the Fifth

Five-Year Plan period (1974–78)! The snail's pace of the government in following up the Wheeler Committee recommendations is underlined by the fact that it was after three years that the report was even tabled at the Central Advisory Board of Archaeology which, in turn, referred it to its Standing Committee. The cavalier manner in which the recommendations were treated comes across when some of the most important ones are juxtaposed with the "action taken" report. The recommendations on "Science and the Survey" is one instance. The Wheeler Committee suggested the setting up of an entirely new kind of archaeological science laboratory which would study building materials and techniques, metallurgy, ceramics and soil samples. This would involve physical anthropology as well as zoology, and so a small scientific advisory committee was also recommended to be formed for consultation. These, the Wheeler Committee underlined, were necessary "if the Survey is to hold its own in the international field…the days have long gone by when contacts between the archaeologist and the scientist were limited to cleaning coins and measuring skulls". The "action taken" report of the ASI, on the other hand, mentioned that the expansion and reorganization of the science laboratory was being contemplated only as part of the Fifth Five-Year Plan. Such a laboratory, incidentally, has still not been set up within the ASI.

A far more comprehensive assessment of the ASI was done by the Estimates Committee of the Lok Sabha in 1973–74.[3] Unlike the Wheeler-led investigation, this committee carefully examined the implementation by the ASI of its own stated projects in the Second Plan period. The preparation of survey plans of monuments, copying of Ajanta paintings and survey of antiquities were among them. The preparation of survey plans, based on local revenue maps, was to be done so that the limits of the protected areas at monuments and sites were demarcated which in turn, would help in preventing encroachment. As the committee pointed out, after more than 15 years, of the 3500 monuments and sites on the Union list, only 525 plans

had been completed in all respects. Nor was the committee convinced by the ASI's reasons that this was due to the non-availability of state government officers for joint inspections. Instead, it opined that this was because of a lack of concerted efforts and follow-up action with the state governments, and urged that effective steps be taken. The same leisurely pace of the ASI was noticed in its project concerning the copying of Ajanta paintings. The paintings to be copied covered 7546 square feet (c. 701 sq. m). The work had been started in 1956–57, and till 1972 the copying of only 2199 square feet (c. 204 sq. m) had been completed. The committee's observation was that "no watch was kept on the progress of work done by the four artists as is evident from the fact that while during the Second Five Year Plan, 1617 sq. ft. of surface was copied by them, which came down to 331 sq. ft. during the Third Plan period and to 612 sq. ft. during the Fourth Plan period".

Exploration and excavation by the ASI came under close scrutiny and it was with some alarm and regret that the committee noted that the number of explorations and excavations had been sharply declining—with 34 in 1969–70, 26 in 1970–71 and a mere five in 1971–72. The ASI's response was that since the Wheeler Committee had suggested that Circle officers devote themselves mainly to conservation work, field research was put on a backburner. The Estimates Committee, however, did not find this to be a satisfactory explanation since an additional Excavation Branch was set up in the Fourth Plan period (1969–74) which ought to have resulted in increased fieldwork. For the expansion of such work, it recommended that the ASI should elicit the cooperation of the state departments of archaeology, universities and research institutes which were carrying on exploration and excavation work. In fact, the report constantly highlighted the urgency of seeking the assistance of universities and other research bodies for partnering the ASI in a variety of projects ranging from an All-India Survey of Antiquarian Remains project to the Temple Survey project.

The theft and smuggling of sculptures and art objects out of India were also matters of concern to the Estimates Committee. The tardy manner in which the ASI had handled the construction of sculpture sheds to protect loose sculptures and antiquities came in for strong criticism. During the Fourth Plan period, apparently, the government had proposed that Rs 10.70 lakhs be spent on constructing sculpture sheds. However, only five sheds were constructed during the first three years of the Plan period (i.e. till March 1972) and a mere Rs 2.70 lakhs of the earmarked amount had been spent. The lack of ASI interest in popularizing archaeology and using it "as a measure of national integration…so that people from one part of the country may learn about the ancient culture of the people from other parts" was another source of unhappiness. In fact, as the committee pointed out, during the five years prior to 1973, only one exhibition was organized by the ASI to display new archaeological finds.

The implications of this excellent report are fairly obvious: the rot in India's archaeological establishment had already set in during the Nehruvian era. In other words, this began before the Wheeler Committee of 1965 did its archaeological review, and that this was not sharply highlighted by that committee may perhaps have to do with the fact that it was headed by an ex-ASI man who may well have wanted to take a charitable view of an organization which he had served and where many of his former students held key posts. On the other hand, the parliamentarians who made up the Estimates Committee of the Lok Sabha presented a far more honest and wide-ranging assessment of the state of the monuments and research under the aegis of the ASI.

Ten years after the Estimates Committee report, the sense of urgency about the decaying state of India's monuments remained, and resulted in the appointment of another committee. Set up by the central government in January 1983, this "Expert Group on Archaeology" chaired by Ram Niwas Mirdha was specifically mandated to "carry out a professional study of the steps that need to be taken and to prepare an overall plan of action in the matter of preserving India's historical monuments in the light of multi-dimensional factors responsible for their damage, especially environmental pollution and vandalism".[4]

In July 1984, the Mirdha Committee submitted its report on what changes were required for the progress of archaeology in general and the ASI in particular. Interestingly enough, because this committee was dominated by former and serving senior ASI officers, there was a palpable attempt to paper over the shortcomings of the ASI. In 1978, for instance, the Central Advisory Board of Archaeology had approved a scheme envisaging 24 national projects, from the Stone Age to the medieval period. The Mirdha Committee noted that as many as ten of these projects had still not been initiated nor was an assessment or review made of projects in progress and the targets achieved. At the same time, we are told, it also observed that "the pursuance of a main objective" had resulted in the discovery of "side issues which are of considerable importance", which therefore made it necessary to redefine goals and lay priorities for addressing specific problems. In other words, unlike the earlier Estimates Committee, no attempt was made here to do a project-by-project audit. Instead, there appears to have been a kind of justification provided for the ASI's laggardly pace of work.

Many of the Mirdha Committee's important recommendations, like those of earlier committees, remained unimplemented. For one, it favoured an all-round upgrading of teaching and research in archaeology in universities, and specifically recommended a delinking from composite departments of "Ancient Indian History, Culture and Archaeology". This has not happened. It also pointed to the absence of planned horizontal excavations and the lack of emphasis on the archaeology of the historical period. Furthermore, it pointed to the threats faced by monuments because of large development projects and recommended that a Salvage Archaeology Wing be set up in the

ASI for properly documenting archaeological wealth threatened by disappearance and submergence. No such wing has yet been set up. The committee's most important recommendation concerned what it perceived should be the status of the ASI: "The Survey should not be considered as a branch of public administration but being an academic institution with highly specialized duties should be accorded a status of scientific and technical institution enjoying autonomy in its functioning like other comparable institutions under the Government." This recommendation was accepted and even officially announced on May 1, 1989. But the notification relating to it was not issued and, thus, it remains unimplemented.

The next intervention was a couple of decades later when in November 2005, the Parliamentary Standing Committee on Transport, Tourism and Culture, headed by Nilotpal Basu, submitted a report to the Rajya Sabha on the functioning of the ASI.[5] The committee report, at the outset, noted that no concrete action had been taken by the Ministry for implementing the notification declaring the ASI as a scientific and technical institution. The committee also regretted the absence of an internal exercise by the Ministry and the ASI for availing the benefits and privileges that accrue to a Science and Technology Department. These remarks, unsurprisingly, fell on deaf ears. Consequently, the ASI continues to function as an attached office of the Ministry of Culture.

The Nilotpal Basu Committee Report recounted a tale of other problems. As it pointed out, for more than a decade, no professional archaeologist had headed the ASI. All director generals during that time period were officers from the IAS cadre. This, despite the fact that in May 2002, an official notification was issued which stated that the ASI's director general should be someone with qualifications and knowledge in archaeology. Eventually, it was some eight years later that an archaeologist was brought in to head the ASI.

The committee's report also chronicled the state of the ASI in some detail. The delay in the publication of excavation reports came in for close scrutiny. By its own admission, at that point of time, of the 292 excavations that the ASI had undertaken since independence, only 45 reports had been published. The most amazing revelation, though, was about the lack of confidence that the leadership of the ASI had in its own cadre. Apparently, when the National Mission of Antiquities was launched in 2005, none of the ASI's officers were regarded as qualified to head such a project. Instead the ASI considered the possibility of handing over this mission to the American Institute of Indian Studies. Why the ASI thought of consciously abdicating its responsibilities still remains unclear, although the implications of such abdication were clearly understood by the Parliamentary Standing Committee. It asked in its report that "adequate care should be taken when finalizing such kind of a deal so that the expenditure to be incurred on the National Mission of Antiquities is spent in the best interests of the nation and valuable information…[is] not handed over to foreign hands". Instead of institution building, the report clearly underlined, outsourcing was becoming a way of solving problems. Outsourcing of its work, incidentally, continues to be done at the ASI.

There is enough in terms of scrutiny and good criticism in the various reports to have helped the ASI, state departments and directorates, museums and the Ministry of Culture to come to grips with the problems facing India's monuments and its archaeological policies. However, the track record of the nodal ministry in killing off recommendations through inordinate delays and postponements has ensured that there is no visible and comprehensive rejuvenation of institutions that are the guardians of Indian archaeology.

Comptroller and Auditor General of India (CAG) Reports

If the above reports highlighted the problems that have dogged the ASI at different points of time, the formidable findings and reports of the Comptroller and Auditor General of India

7.1–7.7 Pages from CAG Report No. 18 of 2013: Performance Audit of Preservation and Conservation of Monuments and Antiquities.

7.1 and 7.2 CAG Report pages 46–47: Management of World Heritage Sites—Taj Mahal, Agra.

Chapter – III : **Management of World Heritage Sites**

We also noticed cracks in the outer walls, broken stones fixed in the wall, missing designs, use of cement in the wall, seepage, fixing of plastic pipes, and broken jalis.

Plastic pipe fixed in the wall **Broken jalis of the outer wall**

Missing stone and plaster

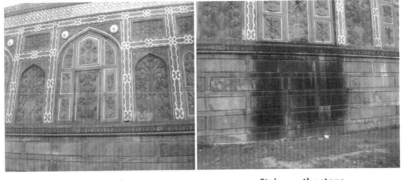

Inlay work   **Stains on the stone**

Garden not maintained

Conservation and preservation works inside the monument were also not satisfactory. The plaster was fading at the main entrance to the monument. There were instances of missing inlay designs and seepage. Even the gardens were not maintained properly.

Garden not maintained   **Missing design**

Performance Audit of Preservation and Conservation of Monuments and Antiquities | 47

7.3 and 7.4 CAG Report pages 79–80: Preservation and Conservation Works—Tripolia Gate, Delhi.

13. St. Angelo Fort, Trissur Circle

During the conservation work carried out in 2000-01, the horse stable originally made of lateritic roof in triangular shape was changed to cylindrical shape roof using cement concrete. The conventional air holes were replaced and its original shape and appearance was drastically changed. This was done despite the prohibition on use of cement concrete on the monuments.

14. Tripolia Gate, Delhi Circle

The work order for special repair work of Tripolia Gate was awarded to M/s AIC Building Solutions Ltd. in July 2010 for ₹ 21.97 lakh with the completion date of 8 November 2010.

In November 2011 during a site inspection, Deputy Superintending Archeological Engineer observed that the plaster work executed by the contractor did not match with the original plaster as the original had various block, moulded and ornamental designs besides floral motif above the arches of Gate. The contractor executed plain plaster work instead of the ornamental designs thus defeating the basic purpose of conservation and restoration. However, the ASI made the payment of ₹ 8.17 lakh. The Circle informed the contractor that the work executed by him had altered the very character of the monument and destroyed the aesthetic view of the monument, which would be difficult to restore at this stage. The Circle asked the contractor to complete the work as per the terms of the Work Order followed by verification by the Deputy Superintending Archeologist. This work had not been corrected till the completion of audit. Thus lack of monitoring by the Circle resulted in improper conservation work by the contractor. The work had not been completed even after a delay of more than 32 months.

Tripolia Gate before conservation

Chapter – IV : Preservation and Conservation Works

Tripolia Gate after conservation (missing designs)

4.5   Preservation and Conservation Works by External Agencies

Conservation is a specialised technical work. Except Delhi Circle, all other Circles of the ASI carried out conservation and preservation work departmentally.   No provision was found either in the ASI Works Code or the ASI Manual for executing conservation work through external agencies in the centrally protected monuments. The Works Code however allowed the ASI to receive funding for conservation work from the external organisations. However, in recent years some external agencies like INTACH, Aga Khan Trust etc. were given monuments for conservation and preservation works. Delhi Circle was getting all its works executed through external contractors.

4.5.1 Monitoring of External Agencies

The ASI had no guidelines regarding engagement of agencies to carry out the conservation works. No laid down criteria regarding the qualification and minimum experience in the related field were fixed by the ASI. In the absence of any laid down criteria, the selection of the agency was done on case to case basis. The following instances with regard to lack of monitoring of the works carried out by external agencies were noticed.

(i)   The ASI entered into an agreement with Aga Khan Trust through NCF in April 1999 for the conservation, research documentation, reinstating of water systems and illumination apart from restoration of gardens of Humayun's Tomb, Delhi Circle. Aga Khan Trust for Culture (AKTC) entered into another MoU in July 2007 with the ASI for the conservation of the protected monuments within the Humayun's Tomb complex. The AKTC was to arrange

(CAG) document in much greater detail the state of India's heritage. The CAG, in fact, has looked at museums and at the ASI in different parts of India. There are important CAG findings that were made public in 2011 relating to several institutions in Kolkata—the National Library, Indian Museum, Victoria Memorial Hall and Asiatic Society.[6] A crucial CAG report was also tabled in the Indian Parliament in 2013.[7] Only a few of the important findings of these reports are discussed here, with some pages reproduced from the 2013 report to illustrate its scope (figures 7.1–7.7).

Considering their long institutional histories, one imagines that there would be uniform benchmarks for the acquisition and care of art objects and antiquities in the government-controlled museums of India. The CAG reports however revealed that frequently the antiquity of artefacts were not properly established by museums before purchase. In one instance, the Purchase Committee of the Indian Museum, Kolkata recommended that two carved pieces of African ivory and a set of chess pieces be acquired merely on a statement made by the individual seller that these artefacts had been collected from African countries by her mother-in-law! There was also no system in any of the institutions to identify damage to objects and to prioritize their conservation. In one instance, the restoration of a batch of oil paintings in the Asiatic Society remained incomplete even after some 18 years. The state of accessioning of objects was even more revealing. Less than 50 per cent of the collection of the Asiatic Society was found to be accessioned in 2004. The state of the Indian Museum was far worse. While in the art and anthropology sections some 88 per cent and 84 per cent of the objects respectively were not accessioned, in the archaeology section the number of accessioned objects was more than the number of objects physically present in this section of the museum.

This institutional malaise exists in the National Museum of India as well, where apparently, at the time of the CAG scrutiny, about a third of its 22 galleries were closed, some like the Manuscript Gallery for as long as eight years. The Art Purchase Committee of the Museum had been defunct for years and an enquiry in 2010–11 showed that the last purchase of art objects was done in 1997. There were also, at that point in time, major safety issues here. The alarm system and the CCTV in the Coin Gallery had not been working from 2007 till 2011 even while regular maintenance charges were being paid for them! Not surprisingly, there had been 156 cases of theft/loss of art objects with 122 in the Anthropology Department and 33 relating to coins. One wonders whether these devastating facts that the National Museum inspection revealed have been adequately addressed.

The CAG in 2013 tabled its "Performance Audit of Preservation and Conservation of Monuments and Antiquities" in Parliament. That report is the most damning indictment of the ASI and the Ministry of Culture in post-independence India—a "monumental" indictment in every sense of the term! And this despite the audit constraints that the CAG faced where many files and records relating to selection of consultants, deployment of security guards, files and records in respect of various monuments were not provided by the ASI and by other institutions that function under the Ministry of Culture.

First, the report comprehensively and publicly highlighted the magnitude of the problem. Whether in relation to monuments or antiquities, the ASI was shown to lack a reliable database. This means that when the ASI says that it protects 3650 monuments, it actually has no such exact figure. A clear example is literally at hand: in relation to Delhi, the ASI headquarters maintained that there were 174 protected monuments whereas the ASI's Circle office listed only 149. The same is true for monuments that have disappeared. Some 35 monuments were reported to Parliament in 2006 as "missing", a number considerably short of the 92 monuments that the CAG recorded as missing.

The bulk of centrally protected monuments, the report noted, had been neglected for years. Those that have received funds appear, with

7.5 CAG Report page 123: Excavation, Epigraphy and Survey—Harappan sites.

Table 5.4 Status of Harappan sites and the antiquities found

Site	Status of the site	Status of antiquities found
Dholavira, Gujarat **Dholavira excavated site**	▪ Site was not fully fenced. ▪ Pottery pieces, beads, earthen bangles, circular buttons, precious stones were lying on the site and were progressively destroyed with visitors walking over it. ▪ A Copper factory and a bead factory found near the excavated site were both under unauthorised cultivation by local farmers. ▪ There were no guide facilities.	A Site Museum with an "Interpretation Cum Information Centre" with 61 photographs of antiquities and 295 objects had been kept. The remaining antiquities were stated to be with the excavation team in Delhi for Report writing work
Rangpur, Gujarat **Site covered with vegetation** **Buildings on the Site** **Archaeological remains on the Site**	The site was not surveyed, measured, demarcated and fenced. Though it was a protected site, the protection notice board, culture notice board were not found. Houses had been constructed on the site. The site was covered under vegetation. Local people were using a portion of the site for taking out soil to make pots and dig ditches.	Artifacts were not collected and kept under safe custody. There was no information available on the antiquities collected at the time of excavation

Chapter – V : Excavation, Epigraphy and Survey

7.6 and 7.7 CAG Report pages 153–54: Management of Antiquities—various museums.

6.14.4 Status of Storage of Art Objects in Different Museums is shown in the following Photographs:

Objects lying in the basement of the National Museum along with other items

Chapter – VI :
Management of Antiquities

Dust gathering over priceless statues in the basement of National Museum

Chapter – VI : Management of Antiquities

Store Rooms of Victoria Memorial Hall

At Benisagar site, Ranchi we found that antiquities were kept in the staff quarters.

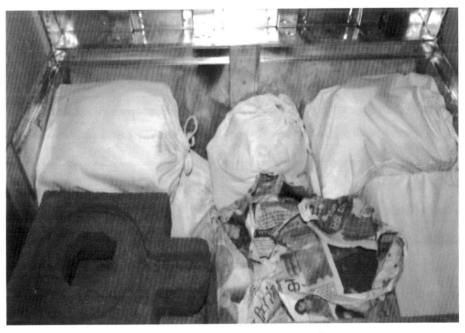

Antiquities found in staff quarters at Benisagar

6.14.5 Storage of Antiquities/conditions of Reserve Items in Site Museums, CAC and Data Bank of the ASI

Proper storage facilities with effective air conditioning and adequate air circulation are essential in order to avoid deterioration of artifacts. We noticed that the reserve collection of Ropar Museum (Punjab Circle) and Fort Museum (Chennai Circle) was not stored in proper condition. Sculptures were lying on the backyard of Aihole Musuem (Dharwad Circle) Chanderi Musuem (Bhopal Circle), Sarnath (Patna Circle) and Nalanda Museum (Patna Circle).

some exceptions, to be poorly conserved. The excellent photographs accompanying the report highlight this fact: several of these are of the Taj Mahal—showing cracks on the outer walls, missing stones and plaster, seepage, and plastic pipes randomly fixed (see figures 7.1 and 7.2). Unauthorized constructions and encroachments are legion, including at World Heritage Sites: 628 at Khajuraho, 194 at Fatehpur Sikri and 107 at Champaner. Preserving excavated mounds is by and large ignored, even the fencing being missing at many sites. Most ASI monuments are without a full-time guard and there is an alarming shortage of technically competent staff.

Exploration and excavation are important responsibilities of the ASI, yet, as the report pointed out, it was spending less than 1 per cent on such work. About a century ago, British India allocated 5 per cent of the archaeological budget for these activities. The writing of excavation reports, as with the Nilotpal Basu Committee, was a matter of much concern to the CAG. These were alarmingly delayed with some pending for more than 50 years (such as those on Mathura, Sravasti and Ropar).

Outsourcing, as the report notes, had adversely impacted the ASI's performance, as the case of inscription of World Heritage Sites demonstrated. When the ASI prepared in-house dossiers, 16 sites were successfully brought within the World Heritage list. However, between 2008 and 2013, when this was outsourced, with the exception of one nomination for the forts of Rajasthan, no other proposals had gone through. On the question of external agencies, the report mentioned a number of instances where there was no monitoring of conservation when these agencies were involved. The World Heritage Site of Humayun's Tomb is an example of this. There, the ASI entered into an agreement with the Aga Khan Trust in 1999 for conservation, documentation, reinstating of water systems and illumination apart from the garden restorations of Humayun's Tomb, and also in 2007 with the Aga Khan Trust for Culture (AKTC) for the conservation of protected monuments within the Humayun's Tomb complex. As the following observation of the CAG underlines, this has resulted in the ASI having abdicated all monitoring in relation to the monument: "The AKTC was to arrange for the funding through domestic or international donors with no financial obligations on the ASI. The Sub Circle in-charge of Humayun's Tomb intimated (January 2013) that he was not aware of terms and conditions of the agreement or the time schedule of the work being carried out by AKTC and thus had no monitoring role. This highlights how the ASI has given up its responsibilities as per the MoU."

Court rulings too were treated with complete indifference. For instance, the Supreme Court of India passed a judgement in 2004 through which notifications issued by the Karnataka government declaring 43 centrally protected monuments as Karnataka Waqf Board properties were annulled. However, the ASI failed to take steps to get the notifications cancelled. In the meantime, the Karnataka government notified six more monuments as Waqf properties in 2005 and this went unchallenged by the Ministry and the ASI.

The scale of encroachments in the case of many centrally protected monuments—by individuals, private organizations and government departments—was alarming. Of the 1655 monuments where records were scrutinized and a joint physical inspection conducted, there were 546 monuments that were encroached. This, incidentally, was more than double the figure given by the ASI to the CAG team. The CAG's observations about this discrepancy are worth quoting: "Evidently, the Sub Circles did not inform the concerned Circle office about the existence of encroachment in the monuments. This indicated that either the monuments were not inspected by the Sub Circle officials periodically or encroachments were made with the connivance of the Sub Circle officials."

These are some of the issues raised in the CAG report that highlight the yawning gap between what is said by the government and what happens on the ground. In 2016, the

Public Accounts Committee of Parliament in its Thirty-Ninth Report gave its detailed observations on the CAG report and the replies of the ASI and the Ministry of Culture, where it expressed deep concern over the state of India's monuments and agencies.[8] In that report, the PAC expressed displeasure over many issues, ranging from the absence of an appropriate and effective mechanism for acquisition of antiquities in the country to the severe shortage of manpower in the ASI. The "lackadaisical attitude" of the Ministry of Culture came in for sharp criticism as also its failure in infusing a sense of direction.

On paper, the Ministry of Culture maintains that "it provides guidance on all policy matters which are implemented by the ASI and the Ministry also monitors the activities of the ASI on all important matters on a regular basis". In practice, there is no monitoring, even when initiatives and projects lie incomplete for decades. This is a ministry living in denial. Surely, as the nodal agency, it has to be seen as squarely responsible for many of the problems and challenges that face India's archaeological heritage today.

Notes

1 Wheeler Committee Report—1965, cyclostyled copy with a covering letter dated April 2, 1965 to M.C. Chagla, Minister of Education.

2 Statement showing Action taken on the Recommendation contained in the Report of the Archaeological Review Committee (1965)—Appendix III in Estimates Committee (1973–74), Fifth Lok Sabha, Fifty-Second Report, Ministry of Education and Social Welfare, Archaeological Survey of India, April 1974, New Delhi: Lok Sabha Secretariat.

3 Report of the Estimates Committee (1973–74), ibid.

4 "Introduction" to *Report of the Expert Group on Archaeology*, New Delhi: Director General, ASI, 1997.

5 Department-Related Parliamentary Standing Committee Report on Transport, Tourism and Culture, Ninety-First Report on Functioning of the ASI, Presented to the Rajya Sabha on November 25, 2005.

6 The reports were sent to me by Atoorva Sinha who directed those audits.

7 Report of the Comptroller and Auditor General of India, Report No. 18 of 2013, Performance Audit of Preservation and Conservation of Monuments and Antiquities, Union Government (Civil): Ministry of Culture.

8 K.V. Thomas (Chairperson), "Protection and Conservation of Monuments and Antiquities", April 2016, Ministry of Culture, Public Accounts Committee (2015–16), Thirty-Ninth Report, Sixteenth Lok Sabha, New Delhi: Lok Sabha Secretariat.

8

Our Heritage and the Law

Safeguarding India's heritage is enshrined in provisions of the Indian Constitution,[1] with both the Union Parliament[2] and State Legislatures[3] being sufficiently empowered to enact legislation (the Union Parliament having the paramount power with respect to monuments that are of "national importance"). There are various legislations that have seen the light of day as a consequence of such provisions. However, as in many areas of public life, the existence of legislation alone is not sufficient. First, citizens have to be ready and willing to comply with laws. Second, authorities must be willing to enforce their provisions. Third, there must be political will to ensure that authorities are empowered to implement such laws. The lack of political will and executive enforcement has forced courts in many instances to either take

suo motu cognizance or entertain a PIL (public interest litigation) to enforce legislation.

There are the thousands of cases that deal with encroachments in the areas of protected monuments or unauthorized constructions around them. In addition, there are some landmark litigations where courts have proactively passed orders to ensure the protection and preservation of monuments. The most significant of these relates to the Taj Mahal in Agra. Finally, a legal milestone of sorts was the excavation that was conducted at the site of Ram Janma Sthan/Babri Masjid at Ayodhya in 2003. This was an unprecedented event in the history of Indian archaeology, because for the first time, the court directed excavations in a case that, legally speaking, was at its core a property dispute.

8.1 and 8.2 Hastinapur— illegal structures on the protected mound. Photographs: Nayanjot Lahiri.

This chapter can only deal with these interventions in an illustrative rather than an exhaustive manner, as it analyses the complex relationship between the law and our heritage, and the tensions located at their crossroads. Hopefully, this survey should provide some sense of the issues that courts have been called upon to decide in relation to monuments and archaeology.

Encroachments, Unauthorized Constructions and Attempts to Change the Status of Monuments

Cases pertaining to encroachments and unauthorized constructions have been and continue to be contested in various states and courts. These relate to a large number of monuments (figures 8.1–8.4 show encroachments on the protected sites of Hastinapur in Uttar Pradesh and Udegolam in Karnataka). This subject has been raised on many occasions in Parliament, and in 2010 the Archaeological Survey of India

went on record to point out litigation arising out of encroachments or physical occupation by unauthorized persons and entities in relation to 249 protected monuments, which had persisted for decades.[4] The CAG Report of 2013, though, mentioned a figure of 546 encroachments in such monuments. The violators involved in ongoing litigations are varied, ranging from individuals to religious boards and even government organizations. A sense of some of these can be had from a list that was compiled by the ASI—constructions by hotels in the prohibited area of "Gada Shah's Shop", Mandu; construction by the Madhya Pradesh Electricity Board in the prohibited area of Sas Bahu Temple, Gwalior; unauthorized constructions by various individuals near Sarkhej monuments, southwest of Ahmedabad; unauthorized constructions within the regulated area of the Shiva Temple at Pali; unauthorized construction work within the protected areas of Jaisalmer Fort and Chittorgarh in Rajasthan;

unauthorized construction by the Church of a prayer hall within the prohibited area of the Chapel of Our Lady of Remedios, Moti Daman.[5] Evidently, First Information Reports (FIRs) filed by the ASI are not proactively followed up by police and district authorities.

There is, however, a more recent twist to this old story. With regard to a dispute around a property in the residential colony of New Delhi's Nizamuddin area, a judgement of the High Court of Delhi in 2009 shockingly revealed that the ASI itself had proactively broken the very law that it sought to defend in various courts against the type of lawbreakers mentioned above.[6] The genesis of the dispute lay in the 1992 notification of the central government, where areas up to 100 metres and areas up to 200 metres near or adjoining protected monuments, as in the case of Humayun's Tomb, were declared to be prohibited and regulated areas respectively. Cases like those mentioned in the previous paragraph, in fact, had arisen out of the infringement of these various zones, which were meant to ensure better preservation and access to the monuments. However, the High Court unearthed an ingenious mechanism through which the ASI had repeatedly broken the law that is supposed to govern these zones.

Apparently, in 2006, the Director General of the ASI prepared a note at the behest of the Minister of Tourism and Culture, for constituting a committee to advise the DG in matters relating to granting permission for "renovation/

reconstruction in the prohibited areas" of protected monuments. For several years afterwards, from 2006 to 2009, such permissions were granted through an Advisory Committee that was specially constituted for this purpose. As the High Court judgement highlighted, it was a matter of grave concern that "the Committee of the ASI, which has no legal basis for its functioning, has been examining applications and granting permissions for construction in 100 m of the protected monuments…without any guidelines whatsoever." Significantly, as it pointed out, this Committee granted permissions for new constructions within the prohibited area and not merely for renovations/reconstructions. All such permissions were held to be illegal and invalid by the High Court. It was as a consequence of this judgement that eventually, in 2010, the Government of India set up a committee which recommended a new Bill to Parliament. It is now known as the Ancient Monuments and Archaeological Sites and Remains (Amendment and Validation) Bill, having been passed by Parliament in March 2010. It is this legislation which has brought the prohibited and regulated zones around monuments within the ambit of the Act itself.

As a consequence of this Act, the National Monuments Authority of India (NMA) was set up to consider applications relating to these zones. It is another matter that even after more than five years, how the NMA functions remains opaque. There is also a marked laxity in relation to one of its major tasks under the 2010 legislation, that of preparing heritage by-laws for nationally protected monuments which are supposed to be placed in Parliament. Instead of preparing those by-laws, the Ministry of Culture recently moved a Cabinet Note which seeks to dilute even the 100-metre prohibited area around nationally protected monuments, by allowing the central government to construct "for public purposes" all kinds of structures there—such as a flyover in the vicinity of Akbar's tomb at Sikandra. Ironically, while the ministers and government functionaries who live in Lutyens Bungalow Zone in New Delhi

have not permitted any overhead metro line in front of their bungalows there, they have no compunction in pushing for a legislation which would allow ugly overhead contraptions in the vicinity of our national monuments. This proposed amendment has now been passed by the Union Cabinet.

Finally, it needs to be pointed out that sometimes the status of monuments, especially religious ones, is sought to be changed. The Sunni Central Waqf Board in Lucknow has been a major actor in trying to change the status of protected monuments in UP. The modus operandi followed by the Waqf Board is to declare protected monuments as Waqf property. Such has been the case with monuments in Agra such as the Moti Masjid, Nagina Masjid, Meena Masjid, the Akbar Mosque in Agra Fort and Jafar Khan's Mausoleum. The demand that the Taj Mahal and its mosque should also be declared Waqf property has to be understood in the light of this context. This kind of registration of "protected monuments" has been challenged by the ASI before the Assistant Waqf Commissioner in Agra and at the High Court in Allahabad on a large number of occasions.[7] What none of the parties involved seems to grasp, however, is that the underlying ownership or property rights in a building or area have no effect on the status of a monument as a protected monument, or indeed on the power of the central government to declare such a monument to be one of national importance, as a proper reading of the Ancient Monuments and Archaeological Sites and Remains Act, 1958 suggests.[8]

Taj Mahal

In some instances, the threat to monuments is of a different order, quite apart from squatters and encroachers. In the landmark litigation described here, the threat that forced the court to act concerned environmental pollution around India's iconic World Heritage Site—the Taj Mahal (figure 8.5).

This arose out of a PIL in the Supreme Court of India in what came to be known as the Taj Trapezium Zone Matter. The court's intervention

8.3 Hastinapur—a statue of the late politician Choudhary Yashpal Singh illegally installed on the protected mound. Photograph: Nayanjot Lahiri.

8.4 Encroachment within the prohibited zone of the Udegolam rock edict of Ashoka. Photograph: Nayanjot Lahiri.

was primarily aimed at mitigating the damage being caused to the Taj Mahal in Agra by the use of coke/coal by industries in the vicinity. After having monitored matters for over three years, with the sole object of preserving and protecting the Taj Mahal from deterioration and damage, the Supreme Court on December 30, 1996 directed all industries operating out of the Zone to start using natural gas as a substitute, and in case they were not in a position to do so, they were to relocate themselves.

The background to this judgement, however, is relevant for understanding how the Supreme Court, in the first place, came to intervene in this matter. It goes back to the decision in the 1960s to set up a refinery at Mathura. A committee was formed to make the precise choice of location from among various alternatives. A number of Chief Ministers lobbied for their states—those of UP, Rajasthan, Haryana and Karnataka. Various locations were examined by the committee and Mathura was eventually finalized—without any thought to the fact that the Taj Mahal was only about 40 kilometres away.[9] Evidently, Mathura was seen as the best choice because of its comparatively superior transport links—it was on a national highway and also on a broad-gauge railway line.

That the Taj was under threat because of atmospheric pollution was known as early as 1971, when an Environmental Impact Assessment Report was prepared by the environmentalist Ashok Khosla. The proposed siting of the refinery at Mathura significantly added to this threat. The ASI clearly was concerned about the pollution impacts of the Mathura refinery on the Taj Mahal as early as July 1973, as several reports had appeared in the press. It is difficult to believe that Prime Minister Indira Gandhi would not have read these reports herself, even if the ASI had not alerted her to the situation. Yet, she allowed the Cabinet to approve the Mathura refinery and personally laid its foundation stone in October 1973 (figure 8.6).

Pollution concerns did not subside after the foundation stone was laid. There were now reports in the international media as well. So, in 1974 the Prime Minister had a committee set up under Dr S. Varadarajan to establish beyond doubt the steps necessary to ensure that the Mathura refinery would not affect the monuments. Having made a wrong choice, Indira Gandhi was going to spare no effort to prevent any adverse fallout. As it turned out, the Varadarajan Committee submitted its "Report on Environmental Impact of Mathura Refinery"

8.5 India's iconic World Heritage Site—the Taj Mahal, Agra. Photograph: Jayant Ugra.

8.6 Prime Minister Indira Gandhi laying the foundation stone of the Mathura refinery, 1973. Courtesy Jairam Ramesh.

in December 1977 by which time Indira Gandhi had left office. The report (published in 1978), forcefully articulated concerns about the threat to the Taj, highlighting that there already was substantial pollution in the Agra region, caused by sulphur dioxide and particulate matter. It identified the pollutants, ranging from power plants to some 250 foundries, and underlined that "efforts may be made to relocate the existing small industries particularly the foundries, in an area south-east of Agra beyond the Taj Mahal so that emissions from these industries will not be in the direction of the monuments." Such concerns were also flagged by the ASI in 1977 which noted that "from the actual deterioration that has occurred on the marble of Moti Masjid inside the Agra Fort and on the red sandstone of the Taj Mahal…the Survey cannot fail to express its deep concern on the possible continued detrimental effect of the present emission and the further additions of pollutants from the Refinery."

Nothing came out of this report in terms of concrete action. The refinery was commissioned in 1982 and consequently, in 1984, the PIL on the Taj Trapezium Zone was filed in the Supreme Court of India where judgement was rendered in 1996.[10] In retrospect, Indira Gandhi's inability to act in this matter sits uneasily with her interest in matters relating to monuments. This, in any case, was no ordinary monument and surely, as an environmentally sensitive person, she was aware of the impact that an oil refinery would have on its larger surroundings. By the time she went to lay the foundation stone of the refinery, Khosla had already submitted his report. One can only surmise that in the tussle between heritage and development, in this instance, she turned her face away from the Taj.

Once the action shifted to the Supreme Court of India, in the course of its hearings, the Court asked for a series of investigations and received several reports—from a variety of organizations ranging from the National Environmental Engineering Research Institute to the UP State Pollution Control Board as also,

once again, from the Varadarajan Committee. In its second report, the comments of the ASI, as cited by the Varadarajan report, clearly mentioned that the studies made by the Science Wing of the ASI "show that suspended particulate matter level has been found to be higher than the maximum permissible level 100 kg/m³. This has imparted a yellowish appearance on the surface of the Taj Mahal."

The Supreme Court judgement recommended that either the 292 industries listed as located and operating in Agra relocate, or they should accept the alternative of using gas instead of coke/coal. As the Court put it, "The atmospheric pollution in the Taj Trapezium Zone has to be eliminated at any cost. Not even one percent chance can be taken when—human life apart—the preservation of a prestigious monument like the Taj is involved."

This judgement was not the end of the matter. In fact, the Supreme Court has since then dealt with the protection of the Taj Mahal on a number of occasions. Ironically enough, its intervention was necessitated because of a lack of political will in many instances on the part of the UP government. In 1998, for instance, it directed an obdurate UP State Electricity Board to sanction 15 kilovolts load for setting up and running the Ambient Air Quality Monitoring Station at the Taj Mahal. As it noted, the Board had treated the ASI Monitoring Station as an "ordinary consumer", thus giving them only 2 kilovolts load, which the Court found "rather distressing" since its whole purpose was to protect the monument.[11] On December 14, 2000, the Supreme Court, as a consequence of the Third Taj Report submitted by the Krishan Mahajan Committee, directed release of funds by the government in order to enable the Forest Department to maintain 1,215,500 saplings—in order to ensure environmental protection around the Taj Mahal.[12] The pollution caused by brick kilns to the Taj was dealt with in 2002 and in 2003.[13]

In 2006, in what is known as the "Taj Corridor Scam Case", the Supreme Court entertained a PIL against the Uttar Pradesh government's Taj

Heritage Corridor Project and prevented the construction of food plazas, shops and amusement activities near the Taj Mahal.[14] In this case, the Court directed a CBI investigation, and it became clear that crores of rupees had been allocated from the UP state exchequer without proper sanction. On the Court's direction, an FIR was lodged by the CBI against the erstwhile Chief Minister of UP, the then state environment minister and several bureaucrats. Chief Minister Mayawati, incidentally, could not be prosecuted because the Governor did not give his sanction for this.

There is little doubt that in a situation where there is a clash between defence of a monument, even one as iconic as the Taj Mahal, and the protection of politicos, heritage is likely to be the loser.

Ayodhya

If it is litigation around protected sites and monuments that has been discussed till now, here I look at an entirely different kind of legal intervention – where the court intervened in order to adjudicate upon a dispute concerning property rights.[15] Archaeology, the judiciary believed, would be able to throw light on whether there was a temple or structure below the Babri Masjid at Ayodhya in UP (figure 8.7) whose wilful and tragic demolition by a well-armed mob on December 6, 1992 was watched on television by the nation and the world.

But, first, some background to this legal intervention is required. This is integrally connected with the dispute over the Ram Janma Sthan mound in Ayodhya. The dispute itself is old. While Muslims claimed the entire premises was a mosque known as the Babri Masjid, since the middle of the 19th century the outer part of the adjoining land had a chabutra (platform) towards the southeast (measuring some 33 sq. m) where Hindus worshipped and which they claimed was much older. Though the dispute was centrally concerned with the different rights and claims of Hindus and Muslims over the site, to begin with this was not about Hindus claiming the spot where the Masjid stood. A

formal physical bifurcation took place there following a riot in 1855. The riot began at another spot, that of Hanuman Garhi, where Muslims had asserted that they had rights because it was previously a mosque. The fighting is said to have extended up to the Babri Masjid site. The Muslims were repelled, and those who died in this riot were buried around the disputed premises. After this, in 1857, a bifurcation was made of the adjoining land by placing a brick and grill wall, dividing it into two parts. Muslims were to use the inner portion while Hindus were to use the outer portion.

Nearly three decades later, a suit was filed in 1885 by Mahant Raghubar Das, of the Ram Janma Sthan against the Secretary of State for India in Council. This suit was for permission to construct a temple over the Ram Chabutra, and for restraining the defendant, the Mutawalli of Babri Masjid, from interfering in the said exercise of the plaintiff. No reliefs, though, were given. The sub-judge of Faizabad noted that while there was no doubt about the possession and ownership of Hindus over the chabutra, near it on the wall of the mosque, the word "Allah" was inscribed. Further, it would be against public policy to permit the construction of a temple because the sounds of bells and the blowing of the shankh by Hindus would create problems for Muslims coming there for prayer and this would lay the foundation of a riot between the two communities. This went up in appeal more than once, but the court judgement was not overturned. Till the end of 1949, prayers were regularly offered by Muslims at the mosque.

It was in November 1949 that there was a strong apprehension that this status quo would soon be overturned. There were reports that a group of Hindus would forcibly try to convert the mosque into a temple. A letter written by the Superintendent of Police of Faizabad, Kripal Singh, to K.K.K. Nayyar, the Deputy Commissioner of Faizabad, clearly articulated this apprehension:

> I visited the premises of Babri Mosque and the Janm Asthan in Ajodhya this evening. I noticed that several "Havan Kunds" have

been constructed all around the mosque. Some of them have been built on old constructions already existing there…. There has been a proposal to construct a very big Havan Kund where Kirtan and Yagna on Puranmashi will be performed on a very large scale…. The plan appears to be to surround the mosque in such a way that entry for the Muslims will be very difficult and ultimately they might be forced to abandon the mosque. There is a strong rumour, that on Puranmashi the Hindus will try to force entry into the mosque with the object of installing a deity.[16]

Within a few weeks of this report, on the night of December 22/23, 1949, Hindus entered the Babri Masjid and placed an idol of Lord Ram below the central dome. An FIR was lodged on the evening of December 23 by Pandit Sri Reo Dubey, Sub-Inspector in charge of the police thana at Ayodhya. He had visited the site that morning and had learnt that a crowd of 50 or 60 persons had broken the locks on the compound of the mosque, placed the idol of "Sri Bhagwan" there, and had written the names of Sita, Ramji etc. on the walls inside and outside in red and yellow paint. Afterwards, apparently, a crowd of 5000 people collected and raised religious slogans and performed kirtan. The idol was placed in the mihrab under the central dome from where on Fridays the imam used to read the khutba (sermon before Friday prayers). From that date, Muslims were not able to offer prayers there.

Until January 1986, the position which was brought into existence on that fateful night of 1949 continued, with two or three pandits deputed to perform bhog and puja and the general public being permitted to have darshan of the idol from the other side of the brick wall. On January 25, 1986, an advocate called Umesh Chand Pandey filed an application that

8.7 The Babri Masjid at Ayodhya, pre-1992. Photograph: Ranjit Sen/Dinodia.

the public must be permitted to have darshan from inside and that the locks placed on the brick grill wall should be removed. The matter was decided within a day of the hearing—on February 1, 1986. The district judge allowed the appeal and the locks were opened. This catapulted the dispute to national proportions. The sense was that justice had not been done. Over the years, the demand for a temple to be built at the site came to be proactively pushed forward by the Bharatiya Janata Party. On December 6, 1992, a large crowd gathered there and demolished the mosque, the boundary wall, the Ram Chabutra etc. in spite of interim orders having been passed by the Supreme Court of India.

Thereafter, the central government acquired a large area of about 68 acres (27.5 hectares), including the premises in dispute, through the Acquisition of Certain Areas at Ayodhya Act 1993. Simultaneously, in its wisdom, it engineered a reference by the President of India to the Supreme Court. The reference was to the following effect: "Whether a Hindu temple or any Hindu religious structure existed prior to the construction of the Ram Janma Bhoomi and Babari Masjid (including the premises of the inner and outer Courtyards) in the area on which the structure stands or not?"

The Supreme Court decided not to answer the reference and, as a consequence of what it said, all the old law suits got revived in UP. It was during the hearings in the Allahabad High Court that it was decided to direct the ASI to conduct an excavation at the disputed site in order to ascertain the previous existence or nonexistence of a temple of any kind at the Babri Masjid site. Following judicial orders, the ASI dug 90 trenches in five months and submitted its report three weeks after the excavations ended, in 2003. As the report observed, "this is an unprecedented event in history of one hundred and forty two years of the existence of the Survey." The ramifications of doing archaeology under court orders are, to put mildly, likely to be wide-ranging. One wonders if this will be cited in future as the precedent for judicial interventions at other disputed sites in

order to support the claims of litigating parties.

After several years, in 2010, a special three-judge bench of the Court comprising Sudhir Agarwal, S.U. Khan and Dharam Veer Sharma pronounced judgement. In a majority of 2:1, it was decreed that there be a three-way division of the disputed land—one-third for the Sunni Waqf Board, one-third for the Nirmohi Akhara and one-third to "Ram Lalla" which was a party in its own right as many deities are. Some months later, this was stayed by the Supreme Court of India.

While I will not comment on the merits of this decision, since the appeal is still *sub judice* before the Supreme Court of India, the judgement of the Allahabad High Court is of tremendous significance to those who have an interest in judicial interventions in matters concerning monuments. On various archaeological and historical points, in fact, there was a divergence of opinion among the judges. By way of example, there was a question concerning the date on which the Babri Masjid in the disputed premises was constructed, and by whom, and its nature. Justice Khan held that it was proved that the constructed portion of the premises in dispute had been built as a mosque by or under the orders of Babur during the period of Babur. Justice Agarwal held that it was not possible to record a finding that the building in dispute had been constructed in 1528. Justice Sharma was of the view that the mosque had been constructed at the site of the old Hindu Temple by Mir Baqi at the command of Babur.

As one looks through the voluminous proceedings and examines the engagements of the judges with religious literature, historical books, gazetteers published in pre- and post-independence periods—as also their examination of a large number of witnesses, including historians, archaeologists and epigraphists—what appears striking is the palpable divergence in the standards applied in the judgement in considering the evidence of expert witnesses. Justice Agarwal, for instance, while considering the statements of expert witnesses in respect of the issue of construction and antiquity of the mosque, not only disregarded such evidence based on minor technicalities, but also seems to have gone to the extent of castigating these witnesses in his judgement. However, in considering the question of whether there had been a pre-existing temple dedicated to Lord Ram at the disputed site, a similar standard was not followed in evaluating the authors of the ASI report of 2003. This was because, unlike historians and archaeologists outside a government organization, these were considered the "experts of experts"!

The troublesome consequences of this clearly point to the problems that result when judgements are based on court-directed excavations that must look for "proof" to help in resolving judicial disputes. The very fact that the excavation was directed by a court of law, and was conducted by the ASI, does not lend any greater credibility to the findings of the ASI in this regard. If courts are to return findings on matters of archaeology and antiquity, they must necessarily be prepared to step into the boots of archaeologists, and analyse competing theories with equal rigour and scepticism, and must also be ready to accept that archaeology does not yield neat, clear-cut answers from material remains.

Notes

1   Article 49 of the Constitution of India.
2   Entry 67, List I, Sch. VII of the Constitution of India.
3   Entry 12, List II, Sch. VII of the Constitution of India.
4   This was formally stated by the ASI to members of the Moily Committee, of which I was a member.
5   "Details of the Court case in respect of the NOC", given to the members of the Moily Committee in 2010.
6   LPA 417/2009, Emca Construction Co. Thr. M.P. Gupta versus Archaeological Survey of India &

others. October 30, 2009 judgement of Chief Justice A.P. Shah and Justice S. Muralidhar.
7   ASI File No. 33/23/89 contains a number of papers relating to this issue.
8   To thwart such illegal efforts at changing the ownership status of monuments, one of the things that the ASI can do is to request the central government to formally acquire the protected monument under Section 13 of the Ancient Monuments and Archaeological Sites and Remains Act, 1958.
9   This paragraph and several others that follow are based on Jairam Ramesh's account of the Mathura refinery case in his forthcoming book, *Indira Gandhi: A Life in Nature* (Simon & Schuster India) the manuscript of which he shared with me, and for which I am very grateful.
10 M.C. Mehta (Taj Trapezium Zone Matter) versus Union of India and Others, (1997) 2 Supreme Court Cases 353, pp. 353–87.
11 M.C. Mehta versus Union of India and Others, (1998) Supreme Court Cases 381, pp. 381–82.
12 M.C. Mehta versus Union of India and Others, Inspection Report of Green Belt for the Month of Nov. 2000 in Writ Petition © 13381 of 1984, decided on December 14, 2000, (2001) 9 Supreme Court Cases 520, pp. 520–21.
13 M.C. Mehta versus Union of India, IAs No. 364, (2012) 8 Supreme Court Cases 132, pp. 131–32; this came up again and orders were passed in 2003.
14 M.C. Mehta (Taj Corridor Scam) versus Union of India and Others, (2007) 1 Supreme Court Cases 110, pp. 110–36.
15 The judgement of the Special Full Bench of the Allahabad High Court in the Ram Janma Bhoomi and Babri Masjid dispute has been published by Malhotra Law House, Allahabad in a set of three volumes (2010).
16 This is from an original file brought to the Allahabad High Court by the D.M. Faizabad. It is cited in the above-mentioned judgement, Vol. 1, p. 36.

9

Antiquarianism and Preservation

So far, this book has concerned itself with protected monuments and their fate, tied up with state agencies and their responsibilities, powers and culpability, as also the interventions of auditors and courts. This final chapter looks at a different kind of universe made up of institutions and individuals who, through entirely different practices, rooted in traditions and customs, protect ancient sites, sculptures and structures. While they do not figure in the legal framework concerning the guardianship of India's archaeological heritage, they have been involved in conserving parts of their material past which give them a sense of identity. The term used to describe such practices is antiquarianism. These people and practices have implications for the survival of unprotected heritage, and their role needs to be highlighted because it has remained entirely unacknowledged in writings on archaeological preservation and protection.

I will first focus on the Ballabgarh region which shares its border with Delhi and forms a segment of the Faridabad district in the state of Haryana, as also Ghaziabad district (in the state of Uttar Pradesh) which lies across the Yamuna from Ballabgarh. In the course of fieldwork in that area, I have had the privilege of observing the various ways in which archaeological relics are understood and collected in many villages there. At the same time, the chapter will also demonstrate that these practices are widely prevalent in other parts of India.

Antiquarian Practices in and around Ballabgarh

The archaeological landscape in Ballabgarh is made up of many elements, from mounds and scatters of artefactual debris to monuments, ruins and sculptural relics.[1] Of these, the collection and preservation of sculptural fragments in villages and their worship in village folk shrines, as a modern practice, is both striking and widespread. Village shrines are of several types. The most ubiquitous are various kinds of grama sthanas (village spots marked by worship) dedicated to a Khera Deota (homestead god)/Khera Dadi (old woman of the homestead) and/or

9.1 Shrine of Sitala Mata in Mawai, Ballabgarh. Photograph: Nayanjot Lahiri.

9.2 Ancient doorjamb worshipped as the Khera Deota in Gharora, Ballabgarh. Photograph: Nayanjot Lahiri.

Bhumia (god of the settled land). These are all seen as manifestations of the inhabited, socially domesticated land and homestead that constitute a village. Architecturally, the shrines tend to be unpretentious, open-air platforms that either have miniature house-like structures, or collections of stone which, in several instances, are broken sculptures from temples of pre-modern antiquity that have now disappeared.

At Mawai, for instance, fragmentary sculptures have been collected and placed in two worship areas. One of these is a Khera Deota shrine opposite the Baba Surdas Mandir where fragmentary sculpted pieces, mainly of mottled Mathura sandstone, have been kept. The other is a shrine of Sitala Mata (the goddess of small-pox) where there are more substantial fragments including a Naga (snake) sculpture, a panel of seven or eight seated figures and the detached sculpture of a full-breasted female torso adorned with three necklaces (figure 9.1).

Another village with an archaeologically significant sculptural collection is Kheri Kalan. Here, on a mound marked by a modern temple and a memorial to a locally revered holy man, there is a Khera Dadi shrine in an open-air sunken enclosure marked by sculptures cemented on to its floor. The identifiable pieces, which range from Shiva lingas and the head of the elephant god Ganesha to the lower half of what seems to be an Uma-Maheshvara image, appear to be generally related to the worship and iconography associated with worship of Shiva (the god of destruction in the holy trinity of Hinduism). Apparently, they were unearthed from the mound where this shrine stands, and underline the possibility that Shiva was the tutelary deity of an earlier shrine here.

In some villages, a single architectural fragment is worshipped. Gharora is one such place, where a section of what seems to be an ancient doorjamb lies on the western edge of the village and is worshipped as the Khera Deota (figure 9.2).

In many places, such archaeological and architectural relics are viewed through a filter of local religious beliefs. Expectations of miraculous cures of ailments, for instance, have come to be embodied in iron slag from the old village mound of Sihi. This place, regarded locally as the birthplace of Surdas, the medieval bhakti poet, is marked by a mound with habitational debris going back to circa 1000 BCE, which yields large quantities of slag. These materials, however, are locally believed to be the "bones" of snakes and are sometimes used as antidotes in ailments caused through poison. What has imbued this residue of early metalworking with a sacred character is its "restitution" within a discourse that is grounded in an old religious tradition. The tradition pertains to a sacrifice that was said to have been conducted by Janmejaya, a king in the *Mahabharata*, the oldest religious epic of India. This was conducted to avenge the death of Janmejaya's father who had been bitten by a serpent king. In the sacrificial fire, thousands of snakes were said to have died through the performance of a serpent-spell and it was locally believed, as it still is, that this sacrifice was conducted at Sihi. That this connection—between an epic event and Sihi's mound—is definitely part of a tradition that circulated in the 16th century is known from, among other things, the testimony of Harirari, author of *Bhavaprakasha*, who is known to have stated that Sur's Sihi was the place where Janmejaya had performed the snake sacrifice. In this way, a local archaeological phenomenon has been interwoven with a textual image of the *Mahabharata*. In the process, it has transformed the meaning that was traditionally read into the epic event (as also into mundane garbage of a past culture) and, through this transformation, it has attempted to create for Sihi an important space in the larger cultural geography of India.

An unusual integration of antiquities into local socio-religious associations can also be seen in the village of Bishrakh in Ghaziabad. Local legend associates Bishrakh with the father of Ravana, the mythical transgressor in the *Ramayana*, the most loved epic of India. Ravana, incidentally, is usually seen as hailing from peninsular India. At Bishrakh, however, unintimidated by the epic tradition, a spot thickly covered with medieval potsherds is pointed out as the place where Ravana was born. The village is situated on a mound with occupation layers that go back to circa 1000 BCE and continue well into the medieval period. From such deposits, a large number of stone Shiva lingas have been recovered, some which are now worshipped in an open-air village shrine, along with a decapitated sculpture of Nandi (the bull vehicle of Shiva). Taken together, these seem to be the remnants of a medieval Shiva temple. Since Ravana is popularly represented as a Shiva devotee, these relics are treated as material evidence for the presence of the mythical villain there. As in the case of village shrines, at Bishrakh too, the valorization of broken sculpture in this way shows how local beliefs can contribute to their preservation.

Such sculptural fragments in Ballabgarh and Ghaziabad, incidentally, form our only evidence for the existence of early Hindu and Jain temples there. To put it another way, these archaeological remnants of ancient "high culture" have become available as a body of historical "evidence" because they are preserved in a dramatically visible way in the arena of modern folk worship. Their worship also speaks volumes for the ground reality and relevance of scriptural sanctions that strictly forbid any worship of broken/mutilated images. Texts like the medieval-period *Pratimanalakshanam* dealing with the creation and installation of images specifically warn worshippers that "the image of a deity, if it be burnt, worn out, broken or split up, after its establishment or at the time

of its enshrinement, will always be harmful. A burnt image brings forth drought, a worn-out one causes loss of wealth, a broken image forebodes death in the family, while one that is split up, war."[2] Unmindful of such proscriptions, broken images are placed on village shrines meant to promote habitational bounty.

From the perspective of archaeological conservation what is most striking is that, by integrating them in their shrines and mythologies, villagers have ensured the survival of ancient artefacts and antiquities in the vicinity of their settlements. This is an excellent and, if I may say so, "non-Western" conservation practice which has ensured the preservation of artefacts and sculpture close to their original contexts. This is not to suggest that destruction of sites and sculpture does not take place in rural India but only to underline that those images and antiquities which are perceived through and incorporated into a filter of local beliefs and practices, are more likely to be revered and preserved. Incidentally, this also holds true for other elements of the landscape, especially trees. A spectacular sacred forest spread over several acres has survived near the village of Mangar in Ballabgarh because of a similar religion-inspired folk tradition, and three villages support and sustain this forest.

Living Antiquarianism in Other Parts of India

The antiquarian practices that I observed in Ballabgarh in the early 1990s, for the first time, made me aware of the little-known ways in which villagers view traces of earlier habitations in their physical surroundings, and how these perceptions have helped to conserve some of those traces. The Ballabgarh experience, in turn, led me to explore, during the course of fieldwork, such practices in other parts of India and to encourage students to examine traces of living antiquarianism in the course of their own research work.

In several villages of north Delhi, for example, a similar practice of collecting and paying obeisance to broken sculpture has been highlighted

9.3 Broken sculpture worshipped either as Bhairon Baba or a female deity in Narela, Delhi. Photograph: Aditi Mann.

9.4 Architectural fragment worshipped as a village deity called Dada Sangla in Mangashpur, Delhi. Photograph: Aditi Mann.

in Aditi Mann's work on the "Archaeology of Religious Worship in North-West Delhi".[3] Sometimes, as her work reveals, these are placed within the premises of temples. Narela is such a village where, in close vicinity of the temple in honour of the goddess Mansa (widely accepted as a manifestation of the goddess Durga), there is a broken sculpture of two figures in a dancing pose. This is clad in a red veil with vermilion sprinkled all over, and is worshipped by some as a female deity, by others as Bhairon Baba (figure 9.3). At Mangashpur village too, the iconic form of a village deity known as Dada Sangla is an old architectural sandstone fragment (figure 9.4). This fragment, embedded in the floor of the shrine, is carved on three sides. One side has a lotus flower in full bloom, another has engraved figures bent over what is perhaps a Shiva linga, while the third side has human figures in a standing posture. Mann, who documented this shrine, is of the view that this is a remnant of an earlier Shiva temple, and she points out that its present worship is also similar to the way in which a Shiva linga is worshipped. On a daily basis, but with the greatest frequency on Mondays, women assemble here and pour water and milk on this fragment.

While Mann's work underlines that in north Delhi's villages sculptural relics can be worshipped as representational forms of deities that bear no resemblance to their original iconic form, this can also be seen in temples at major centres of Hindu pilgrimage. Some three decades ago, the bell capital of an Ashokan pillar was "discovered" in the Nageshwar Nath Temple at Ayodhya (Uttar Pradesh) where it was, and continues to be, used as the base on which the Shiva linga in the temple is worshipped.[4] That this capital crowned a pillar that, more than two millennia ago, was set up on the orders of an emperor with strong Buddhist inclinations, evidently does not matter either to the devotees or to the caretakers of the temple. However, because it has been integrated into the paraphernalia of worship there, it has survived.

Moving away from the north, motley groups of sculpture in shrines of worship exist at a

9.5 Images placed in niches of the boundary wall of the Maruti Temple in Kayatha, Ujjain district. Photograph: Nayanjot Lahiri.

number of places south of the Vindhyas, and I have documented many such instances in Madhya Pradesh. In several places, such collections are in the precincts of temples. What is particularly striking is that, at first glance, they seem to be displayed in an open-air museum-like arrangement in shrines, lined along the shrine precincts or placed in niches. Unlike museums, however, they are often secured with cement into walls and niches.

An outstanding exemplar of this tradition is the Maruti Temple at Kayatha in Ujjain district, dedicated to the god Hanuman. Kayatha is a village located on ancient mounds on the right bank of the Chhoti Kali Sindh river. Excavations in the 1960s revealed here a sequence of cultural periods going back to circa 2000 BCE. The site continued to be inhabited till circa 600 CE which is also the time period when the celebrated astronomer of India, Varahamihira, was believed to have been born at Kayatha. The archaeological discovery of this site and its significance are recorded in the form of a long inscription that is prominently displayed in the Maruti Temple, a modern record that is remarkably rare in village

shrines. What is even more interesting is that a number of architectural fragments and images have been secured in the niches that line the boundary wall, or that part of it which demarcates the approach route to the temple (figure 9.5). The most well preserved of the Kayatha sculptures is a medieval lifesize image of Vishnu which, in fact, has been kept on the temple platform itself.

Such curious antiquarian collections I have encountered in other parts of India. In the city of Ujjain, for example, at the Vikrant Bhairav Temple, a large quantity of sculpture has been kept in much the same way as at Kayatha (figure 9.6). Vishnu and Shiva images along with Shiva lingas and architectural relics are built into walls and the floor of its courtyard. Similarly, a few hundred kilometres away, in the remote town of Narsinghgarh (Rajgarh district), the local Shiva Temple has preserved old sculpture by building pieces into the walls that demarcate the shrine as also into the walls that fringe the steps leading up to the temple. Worship of stray sculptures lying around fields or on a hillside is fairly common all over the country (figures 9.7–9.9).

On occasion, temples can also have storehouses attached to them where sundry images and sculptural pieces are collected, stored, and sometimes displayed and worshipped. This is especially visible, as a living practice, in Jain temples. The historical sense of the Jain community, incidentally, is well known from its tradition of collecting handwritten manuscripts in bhandars (warehouses). These manuscripts are seen as a means of preserving Jain knowledge, and some bhandars in Rajasthan and in Gujarat are known to have as many as 10,000 manuscripts and books in their collections. The establishment of bhandars is widely documented in the medieval centuries, when Jain kings and merchants established libraries, and some of those libraries still exist as, for instance, the Shri Hemachandracharya Jain Jnananmandira in Patan, with manuscripts that go back to the 15th and 16th centuries.[5] Interestingly, manuscripts and books in libraries and bhandars are worshipped as sacred objects once a year on the fifth day after the advent of the New Year known as Jnan Panchami ("Knowledge Fifth")—with hymns and offerings.

Much less known than the collections of manuscript and books in bhandars is the practice of keeping old architectural and sculptural paraphernalia in storehouses and worship areas of Jain temples. An excellent example of this is Shantinath Digambar Jain Temple in Hastinapur (Meerut district, Uttar Pradesh). Built in the early part of the 19th century, some of the old images are under worship. Two of these are kept in the main sanctum sanctorum along with several newer ones, and there are old images in a subsidiary shrine there as well. Most significantly, the temple has a small museum (which is presently under renovation) where there is a collection of bronze images, carved stone panels with multiple Jina representations, as also old religious photographs and paintings (figure 9.10). Similarly, at another Jain temple—the Sahastra Kuta Jinalaya—in the nearby Jambudvipa complex, an old panel depicting a Jain monk has been placed in the worship room where the central Jina panel that is the real object of worship here, stands. This panel was apparently discovered when the foundations for the construction of the Jinalaya were being dug.

9.7 and 9.8 Naga sculpture (front and back) under worship on Nagauri hill adjacent to Sanchi. Photographs: Nayanjot Lahiri.

The Shantinath Digambar Jain Temple is at least 200 years old. This practice, though, can be seen at newer Jain shrines too. One of these is the Shri Atman Vallabha Smarak located on National Highway No. 1. The Smarak is very close to Delhi, on the way to Chandigarh, and was constructed in 1984 by the followers of Vijay Vallabh Suri, a Jain Acharya who spent most of his life preaching in Punjab.[6] This, however, is more than a temple and contains a small valuable collection of medieval manuscripts and images. The images and sculptures—of tirthankaras/jinas as also of the mother goddess Ambika, and panels of yakshas and yakshis—are displayed in the temple basement. These constitute what another Acharya, the late Nityanand Suri, along with a few other monks searched out of remote villages and small towns. The images

are mainly from places in Gujarat, Rajasthan and Maharashtra that boast of important Jain mercantile groups. As in old antiquarian collections, such sculpture has been, without any sense of incongruity, kept alongside the personal belongings of Acharya Vijay Vallabh. The Acharya's clothes, utensils, even his dentures and the inkpot that he used are showcased in the same space as Jain images and panels!

Collecting and preserving antiquities and sculpture in religious shrines and spaces is evidently a widespread practice. The collections of artefacts, sculpture and architectural pieces in religious places of worship—in and around village shrines and city temples—are sometimes the only clues that have survived about their antique pasts. This practice therefore needs to be integrated into our understanding

9.9 A Kanaganahalli sculpture being worshipped in the fields nearby. Photograph: Nayanjot Lahiri.

9.10 Stone architectural piece showing multiple Jina representations, kept in the "museum" of the Shantinath Digambar Jain Temple in Hastinapur. Photograph: Nayanjot Lahiri.

and appreciation of the different ways in which ancient paraphernalia has survived in modern India.

Notes

1   The references to my publications on Ballabgarh are available in Nayanjot Lahiri, "Living Antiquarianism in India", in Alain Schnapp (ed.), *World Antiquarianism: Comparative Perspectives*, Los Angeles: Getty Research Institute, 2013, pp. 423–38.

2   Jitendra Nath Banerjea, *The Development of Hindu Iconography*, New Delhi: Munshiram Manoharlal, 1956 (reprint), p. 615.

3   Aditi Mann, "Archaeology of Religious Worship in North-West Delhi", MPhil dissertation, University of Delhi, 2011.

4   This was discovered by R.S. Bisht. See Swaraj Prakash Gupta, *The Roots of Indian Art*, New Delhi: B.R. Publishing Corp., 1980, p. 27.

5   John E. Cort, "The Jain Knowledge Warehouses: Traditional Libraries in India", *Journal of the American Oriental Society* 115(1), 1995, pp. 77–87.

6   Aditi Mann, "On National Highway No. 1, a Slice of Secret India", *Hindustan Times*, July 26, 2008, p. 18.

Epilogue: Making Heritage Matter

India's archaeological inheritance has continued to grow in many different ways since independence, even as our rich heritage of monuments and relics, sites and sculpture remains vulnerable and compromised. This is far too fragile to be left to pious posturing about its beauty and greatness. A sense of its ownership at the highest echelons of government and across all sections of society is urgent and necessary if it has to survive in a better form than what we see around us. This will require improvements in the quality and direction of commitment and communication, both among people in the profession of researching the past and protecting monuments, and from them to other audiences. In this concluding section, I offer my own observations on how India's heritage can be made to matter more than it does at present.

To begin with, heritage conservation as it is presently undertaken needs to undergo a major overhaul. The deplorable deterioration of both the principles and standards, in spite of increasing amounts of government money being spent on structural and chemical conservation, underlines that it is not the lack of resources but of accountability that is responsible for the present state of affairs. There is no universally agreed protocol for conservation in India, with the same government department doing different things at different sites.

The corruption that conservation work has generated is also worth addressing. In fact, conservation weighs like a millstone on the neck of the ASI, where its personnel are more concerned with the remunerative aspects of conservation than with anything else. There should be a powerful body vested with overall conservation responsibilities on the lines of a National Heritage Commission. Certainly, such a body should be integrally engaged with government departments in relation to the archaeological aspects of monuments and sites, but the ultimate responsibility for ensuring that respectable standards of conservation are maintained should rest with it.

The regulatory framework that a National Heritage Commission puts in place ought to be more decentralized. Specifically, it should evolve ways of institutionally integrating municipalities and village panchayats in heritage conservation and management work. Village- and district-level repositories where local material is displayed and conserved should be created. It is, after all, villagers who have frequently ensured the survival of ancient artefacts and antiquities found in the vicinity of their settlements. Surely, 70 years after independence, state policy should not be informed by the same logic that was deployed by the British against India—that India's heritage had to be saved from its own people. A system in which community groups as heritage managers work in partnership with the State is also likely to produce more positive results than the present system of conservation. This is because historic landscapes have a better chance of survival if those who inhabit or live in the vicinity of these landscapes have responsibilities and a participatory role in their management and use.

Heritage laws also need to be re-examined. The plethora of central and state legislation, as it exists, has failed to adequately protect our heritage. Has enough thought gone into understanding whether these laws conform to the ground-level situation? The legislation pertaining to antiquities, for one, needs to be more realistic and transparent, if it is to be enforceable. It has to become more people-friendly. The observations of the archaeologist Dilip Chakrabarti on the draconian nature of the Antiquities and Art Treasures Act of 1972 are worth quoting:

> It is draconian in the sense that it virtually makes the possession of an antiquity by a god-fearing Indian a criminal offence. The

Sculptures and images kept in the vicinity of the hill where they were discovered near Tekkalakota. Photograph: Nayanjot Lahiri.

onus of registering everything with the government and that too in triplicate, with three copies of photographs and within a very short time-frame lies entirely with the individual. In a country with limited literacy the effectiveness of such a piece of legislation can easily be imagined![1]

Further, the present legislations are silent on protecting historic landscapes. Monuments and structural ruins are parts of landscapes which in many regions of the world are now treated on par with them. The accompanying photograph of sculpture near Tekkalakota in Karnataka with the backdrop of the rocks makes for a wonderful ambience, and reveals how important it is to allow structural elements to remain in their original surroundings as also to ensure that such surroundings remain untouched by "development". There are, however, no provisions for protecting the surroundings. So, for instance, in an area like Mehrauli where there are numerous protected structures, there is no provision for protecting the already endangered Aravalli landscape. Across that entire terrain are numerous scatters containing remnants of Stone Age humans, the first inhabitants of Delhi. There is, however, nothing in the current legal framework which provides effective protection to such landscapes. Consequently, most of them have been destroyed.

It is unlikely that the current framework can cope with the impact of accelerated industrialization, especially the creation of Special Economic Zones (SEZs) in different parts of

India. Certainly, since independence, salvage archaeological work has sometimes helped mitigate the collateral damage that accompanies development. For instance, we have seen how Nehru ensured that the Nagarjuna Sagar dam construction was combined with an excavation and rescue project at the site of the historic Ikshavaku capital of Nagarjunakonda. But are there structural safeguards in place when large projects like SEZs over thousands of hectares are sanctioned, or when the creation of communication corridors for rapid transit projects like the metro rail are undertaken? The environmental impact assessment does not make it mandatory for large projects to get the dedicated land vetted and documented by archaeologists. Surely, this should be done. Additionally, the reservation of a certain percentage of the estimated cost of a big project should be made mandatory—for the purpose of an archaeological documentation of the area before construction. This is done in many parts of the world even in situations where the archaeological and built heritage only goes back to a couple of centuries ago.

A comprehensive approach to our heritage involves more than conservation and restoration. The ramifications of what is happening in the field and, more than that, the necessity of assessing the already existing and newly emerging field data in terms of their significance, need to be addressed. Also, while there is a great deal of available information of different aspects of India's heritage, little has been done to use this either for policy initiatives or for creating public awareness. None of the major policy research centres had thought of it as a priority area worthy of intervention.

Above all, information generated by scholars and agencies about India's archaeological heritage must be made available. Archaeological knowledge, as V. Selvakumar has pointed out, should be communicated as widely in publications in the vernacular languages, in the same way as it is presently done in English.[2] One may add that such knowledge should be integrated in a practical way into school teaching. It wouldn't cost anything for teachers to teach history while making students imbibe their local heritage firsthand, since in practically every nook and corner of India there are mounds, monuments, sculptural relics and lots more. Simultaneously, it is time that professionals and experts outside government regularly prepare reports on the "State of India's Archaeological Heritage". Assessments of many spheres of government are regularly made; these help articulate policy and legislation. If the exercise is extended to monuments and sites, it would help generate pressure on those who are paid to preserve our past.

The more pressure that is generated on the institutional guardians of India's archaeological heritage, the more likely it is that these guardians would cease living in denial. Surely India's archaeological heritage, 70 years after independence, deserves better than what has fallen to its lot.

Notes

1 Dilip K. Chakrabarti, *Archaeology in the Third World: A History of Indian Archaeology Since 1947*, New Delhi: D.K. Printworld (P) Ltd., p. 182.

2 V. Selvakumar, "Public Archaeology in India: Perspectives from Kerala", *India Review* 5 (Nos. 3 and 4), July 2006.

Nayanjot Lahiri is Professor of History at Ashoka University, Sonepat, Haryana. She established her reputation as an accessible historian of Indian antiquity with *Finding Forgotten Cities: How the Indus Civilization Was Discovered* (2005). Her other books include *Marshalling the Past: Ancient India and its Modern Histories* (2012) and *The Archaeology of Indian Trade Routes* (1993). She was awarded the Infosys Prize in Humanities—Archaeology for 2013, and her most recent book *Ashoka in Ancient India* won the John F. Richards prize of the American Historical Association for the best book in South Asian History for 2015.

Index